From the Ends of the Earth

Kathryn Kerridge

From the Ends of the Earth

Copyright © 2010 Kathryn Kerridge

Scripture quotations marked NLT are taken from the Holy Bible, New Living Translation, copyright 1996, 2004. Used by permission of Tyndale House Publishers, Inc., Wheaton, Illinois 60189. All rights reserved.

Scripture quotations marked NIV are taken from the Holy Bible, New International Version, copyright 1973, 1978, 1984 by International Bible Society. All rights reserved.

Scripture quotations marked NKJV are taken from the Holy Bible, New King James Version, copyright 1990, 1985, 1983 by Thomas Nelson, Inc. All rights reserved.

All rights reserved. No part of this publication may be reproduced, stored in a retrieval system or transmitted in any form or by any means, electronic, mechanical, photocopying, recording or otherwise, without the prior written permission of the publisher.

The information, views, opinions and visuals expressed in this publication are solely those of the author(s) and do not reflect those of the publisher. The publisher disclaims any liabilities or responsibilities whatsoever for any damages, libel or liabilities arising directly or indirectly from the contents of this publication.

A copy of this publication can be found in the National Library of Australia.

ISBN: 9781921681547 (pbk.)

Published by Book Pal
www.bookpal.com.au

Dedicated to my dear parents,
Max and Margaret Kerridge,
two of my 'heroes of the faith'.
Without their love, prayers, support and example,
I would not be where I am today.

I love you!

'I remember the days of old.
I ponder all Your great works
and think about what You have done.'
(Psalm 143:5 NLT)

'My purpose in writing is to encourage you ...'
(1 Peter 5:12 NLT)

Foreword

There lived an Australian girl for whom life looked very good.

Five years of university study in the fields of Arts and Law were finally completed and the next stage of her legal career had commenced with a job in a city law firm. The girl was twenty-two.

She had loving family, great friends and by all accounts a promising future living under the tropical Queensland sun.

The girl also had a deep faith in God, having been a Christian since the age of about five. From her faith flowed the belief that life on this earth had a much higher purpose than having a good time, being comfortable and accumulating 'stuff'. It was her greatest desire to live a life that was pleasing to God and a blessing to others, and to point people towards Christ in all that she did.

Active involvement in church, youth group and volunteer work was a natural overflow of her spiritual life and an effervescent personality. Passionate about working with children on Christian holiday camps, the girl delighted to show them and tell them how special they were, and how much God loved and valued them.

Hopes and dreams for the future were cherished in her heart, although the girl did not expect life to be a smooth ride all the way. God as her loving heavenly Father had a purpose and a plan designed just for her, the girl believed. Whatever that future held, He would be with her to guide, help and protect her every step of the way.

And then everything began to fall apart.

Within a few months, the girl's whole world collapsed, and the future that once looked bright became bleak, a dark cloud of hopelessness and despair.

The ensuing events felt like a violent ambush – it was as if she was falling into an endless abyss, desperate for something to cling to, terrified, crying out for help. Everything that she had known and believed was shaken to the very foundations.

Instead of really living, it seemed she was barely surviving. Breathing merely to exist in a daily fog of indescribable fatigue, pain and depression. Praying that she could somehow fall asleep and never wake up. Anything to bring an end to what seemed a completely futile existence.

Most terrifying of all to her was the fact that God seemed to have completely vanished. She felt abandoned, bewildered, frightened, hurt, angry – as if she had been left to face a horrible fate alone.

Could it be possible that this faith upon which she had built her whole life was a farce ...even a lie? What had been the point of any of it? What was the point of anything now?

Although she wondered if she would, or even if she wanted to, survive, the girl nevertheless did. It was not an easy process and the crushing circumstances did not disappear, but the girl came to understand more profoundly and believe even more deeply that the God of the Bible does exist and is who He says He is. He is ever present even when He *seems* absent, and He is able to bring about beauty from a life left in ruins.

Serving God in whatever way she could was the girl's main aim in life. She had feared that the collapse of her body and life had rendered her useless for His purposes. Instead, it actually opened up more possibilities than she ever could have planned or imagined for herself.

To this very day, the circumstances that brought about this crisis of life and faith remain, but the result has been anything but a static and ruined life – far from it, in fact. With a restored faith in God, a backpack, and a travel guidebook in hand, the girl has since travelled the globe, led by God and used by Him to share her faith and the hope that she has. She has seen God take care of the big stuff in the overall picture of her life. She has seen God take care of the tiniest details that only He could know and care about. She has watched in amazement and humility as her life has been rebuilt and her character shaped through the fire of refining – and she regularly finds herself open-mouthed with awe and humbled with deep gratitude to the God who didn't give up on her...even when she was very close to giving up on Him.

This is the story of that life. It is not the most extraordinary life story in the world; it is not the most dramatic; it is certainly not the most painful. Like the stories of most other lives, it is composed of joy, sorrow, laughter, pain, friends, family, school, work, faith...the everyday stuff of life, really.

It *is* a story of how God takes the ordinary, everyday events, the random jigsaw pieces that seem unimportant...or coincidental...or meaningless...or senseless..., and builds them slowly (and sometimes painfully) into a picture of incredible detail and beauty. The problem is, only He has the jigsaw puzzle box which displays the finished picture. It is left to us to trust that He knows what He's doing.

God cares about the big picture of a person's life. He alone knows the steps that are necessary to lead to the end result only He can always see. However, God is also a master of detail. As well as providing guidance and help in life's big issues, He is also mindful of our needs, our cares, our dreams, what makes us laugh with exultation, what makes us cry with anguish; nothing is too small to escape His attention.

If you have ever suffered a devastating illness and wondered where God was in the pain; if your life has ever taken a violent about-turn which left you reeling; if you have ever felt too weak or too inadequate to be of any use to God; if you have ever wondered about the type of person God calls to do mission work; if you have ever wondered what it means to live a Christian life which includes God in everything; even if you are just wondering how the girl's story ends, keep reading!

God cares about you more than you can possibly know – He's in the big stuff and the little stuff every day, and I pray that you will see those truths in the story of one ordinary girl's life and realise that they can be true in yours too.

From the Ends of the Earth

Chapter 1

I was born in November 1970 to Max and Margaret Kerridge, a Christian couple who had been married for almost a year. Their first experience of parenthood was not an easy one – poor Mum suffered awful morning sickness for the whole pregnancy, and then I gave them quite a fright when I was born six weeks premature, weighing only about four pounds.

Four pounds sounds almost robust when compared with today's fragile babies who survive much more premature births, but in 1970 my situation was quite serious and survival was not a foregone conclusion. I was very ill, needing a total blood transfusion, and spent about a month in a hospital humidicrib before my parents were able to take me home. I was allowed home when I reached five pounds in weight only because Mum had been a nurse.

Hour upon hour, Dad would pace the floor at home, carrying me cradled on a pillow as I cried incessantly through many a night.

I could so easily have died at birth or soon after – but I didn't. God had kept me alive – although there was a time much later on in my life when I would wonder why He had bothered.

Kathryn Kerridge

I was born into a long and solid Christian heritage on both sides of my family, and this influence was to be instrumental in the formation of my own faith and the shape that my life would take. My birth, although unplanned by my parents so early on in their marriage, was certainly no accident in God's grand scheme of things, and that included His placement of me in this particular family.

My father's parents, Wes and Madge Kerridge, lived at Stanthorpe in south-west Queensland where my grandfather was a farmer.

When WWII broke out, Grandpop enlisted in the army and was sent as a signalman with troops going to battle the Japanese in Asia. Three and a half of his five years away were spent as a prisoner of war in the infamous Changi prison in Singapore. He was among soldiers forced to work on the 'Death Railway' and at one stage was treated by Edward 'Weary' Dunlop, an army doctor who became an Australian hero for his services to soldiers in the POW camps.

This was a time of great uncertainty for my grandmother. For a while, Grandpop was listed as 'Missing in Action' and Grandma didn't know whether he was alive or dead. In those years of limbo, she moved to live with her mother at Palm Beach on the Gold Coast, and concentrated on bringing up her only child, a snowy-haired little boy called David Maxwell (Max), my father.

From the Ends of the Earth

Miraculously, Grandpop survived those years of shocking malnutrition, tropical diseases and inhumane treatment, and, after the Allied liberation of Singapore, was eventually repatriated back to Australia. Dad was so young when his father left for the war that he could only identify his dad from a photo, and although he knew his dad was a soldier, didn't really 'meet' him properly until he was between six and seven years old.

Just as miraculous in my eyes as his survival is the fact that my grandfather refused to allow bitterness to poison his life. He never talked about the war years – in his mind, what was past was past – and although he was understandably forever affected and hardened in certain ways, I remember him as hard-working, loving and faithful to his family and to God, active in the church and generous towards others. He managed to write some secret diaries in the POW camp, secreting them in a little waterproof pouch, but it wasn't until Grandma found and transcribed them after Grandpop had died that we had any real idea of what he had suffered.

After the war, Grandpop and Grandma, with little Max, moved to Wellington Point. In this beautiful bayside suburb of south-east Queensland, which was blessed with rich, fertile red soil, Grandpop resumed farming. Five other children were subsequently born, and the family was raised in a Christian environment, attending church together regularly. However, a parent's faith is not automatically transmitted to their children. An individual personal decision has to be made and Dad made a commitment as a teenager to follow Christ.

My mother was born in England to an English mother and an Australian father. Sensing a call to serve God through the China Inland Mission, Charles Frencham and Ruth Wheatley applied to do so independently from opposite sides of the world. They met and married in China, and during their years of service had five children.

A girl and a boy were born in China, and during a furlough in England, another baby girl arrived. This middle child was my mother, Margaret Ruth, born in Burgess Hill in West Sussex, which was also the birthplace of my grandmother. After their return to China, two more children, both boys, were born.

During Mao Tse Tung's Long March in 1935, Grandma and Grandpa Frencham were captured and held by communist guerrillas, Grandma being heavily pregnant with her first child at the time. On three separate occasions they were taken outside to be shot, but each time their captors inexplicably relented. After six weeks of captivity, they were released. Grandma had managed to hide her precious gold wedding ring by weaving it into her long black hair, which she wore in a bun.

Soon after the birth of Mum's youngest brother, the family left China. Burgess Hill was to be their home

From the Ends of the Earth

for the next eight years, after which they emigrated to Victoria, Australia, Charles' birthplace. In 1953, at the age of fifteen, my mother with her family boarded a ship at Tilbury Docks in London to embark upon the six week voyage to Australia. As she boarded the ship 'Otranto', accompanied by her one little trunk of belongings, my mother never knew if she would set foot in her homeland again. At the age of eleven, Mum had made a personal decision to follow Christ, and her faith would prove a source of strength and help as she started a new life in a foreign land.

No one knows exactly what atrocities my grandparents suffered at the hands of their communist captors – no one even knows to this day why they were even released, except that many people were praying. My grandfather later suffered a stress-related condition and subsequent family life was far from easy. Despite this, faith and trust in God remained the highest priority in their home, and my grandmother in particular was known by all for her incredibly loving, sweet and gentle nature. After their immigration to Australia, my grandparents continued to live in Victoria until their death.

After arriving in Australia, my mother completed a general nursing qualification in Victoria and then moved to Brisbane in Queensland for midwifery and maternal and child welfare training. She lived in nurses' quarters but had an 'adopted' family in Cleveland. She attended the Presbyterian Church there on Sundays, where she was soon noticed by my dad at the services.

After a first date at the cinema to see 'The Ten Commandments' (!), romance blossomed, and they were married on January 3, 1970. Although the plan was to wait a while before having children, before they knew it, I was on the way. Impatience was obviously one of my earliest visible traits!

After a cursory glance at my family history, it is perhaps no surprise that faith in God combined with travel around the world would play such key roles in my life. I guess someone in our family was destined to inherit missionary genes…I just didn't expect it to be me!

Chapter 2

Despite my rather traumatic start in life, my childhood growth and development progressed as expected. I walked comparatively late, and seem to have completely skipped the crawling stage, preferring instead to 'swim' along the floor on my stomach until one day I clambered to my feet. However, I mastered talking earlier than most, which will come as no surprise to those who know me! Finding it a little difficult to articulate my name, I dubbed myself 'Cha-Cha'. Apparently I would often refer to myself in the third person, as in, 'Cha-Cha will have some, please, Mummy!' As I grew, it was apparent that I had suffered no long term physical or mental ill-effects of my difficult birth and early months.

Two and a half years after I was born, a little brother, Andrew, arrived on the scene to complete our family. Dad was a farmer like his father (although we ourselves didn't live on a farm) and he worked long, hard hours from dawn till dark, six days a week. Mum stayed at home to look after Andrew and me.

Our childhood was a happy and secure one. It wasn't perfect, and Andrew and I certainly engaged in regular bursts of sibling conflict, but we grew up in a home full of love and were well provided for materially, emotionally and spiritually.

Kathryn Kerridge

Due to Queensland's wonderful tropical and sunny climate, we spent huge amounts of time outdoors. Houses were roomy and detached with backyards and garages, so there was always plenty of space to run around and play. With abundant sunshine and almost the same number of daylight hours all year round, our free time was generally spent playing cricket or on the swings in the backyard, riding our bikes around the streets, swimming in our friends' pool, and building cubby houses in trees.

In fact, our backyard must have been a big eye-sore most of the time...a set of cricket stumps had its permanent place in one section, and well-marked creases had scared away any grass that might have been tempted to grow there. The guinea pigs munched their way down another strip of the backyard. Dad never mowed this section so there was always a fresh supply of greens for our pets. By the time the cage was moved bit by bit to the bottom of the yard, the grass at the top had grown again.

For a decade or so, a cubby house of one design or another was constructed in the lower branches of one particular tree, perfectly shaped for the purpose. Poor dad, farmer and gardener extraordinaire, was faced with the sight of trampled ferns underneath it, planks and platforms of wood nailed onto it, and the decorative effects of old tarpaulins, blankets, little cupboards and an array of other features adorning it. One day when I was about ten, Andrew and I were in the cubby munching our way through a packet of barley sugars. (We were participating in the World Vision 40-Hour Famine at the time but never quite understood that a barley sugar was allowed instead of a meal if you needed an energy boost. You weren't supposed to fill up on them!) All at once we heard an ominous cracking sound, and the next thing we knew we were sitting on our cubby floor on the ground! The poor tree had finally had enough of our construction experiments. We gave that tree a rest for a while and turned our attention to another one.

In the heat of summer, we'd cavort under the lawn sprinkler in our togs (swimsuits) or sometimes make our own 'slip and slide' using the hose, a tarpaulin and lots of dishwashing liquid. A summer rainstorm need never be wasted – newspaper would be transformed into paper boats to race down the gutter of the street – sometimes it was very handy to live in a house on a hill.

Various combinations of cats, budgies, finches, fish, mice and guinea pigs were part of the family line-up and looking after them was part of our daily chore list. Pippy and Fluffy, the guinea pigs, were bathed regularly. In summer, a bath cooled them down, but in winter their fur had to be blow-dried to prevent them catching cold. Yes, the Kerridge pet beauty salon was a popular Saturday afternoon destination. What better pampering but a relaxing shampoo and massage, followed by a gentle rub-down with a towel then a blow-dry and set. We tried to bathe the cat once (with a flea solution) but he didn't even stick around long enough to get completely wet, let alone anything else.

Andrew and I were lovingly and well provided for by our parents, but we were not indulged and were disciplined appropriately, too. On reflection, we were certainly 'spoilt' on occasions, but we also had to do chores to earn our pocket money, could lose 'privileges' (such as TV time) for misbehaviour, and were taught the value of money by having to save to buy Christmas or birthday presents for others, or lollies at the corner shop, or extra toys or books that we wanted.

I was a pretty good kid, really, but I was no saint – I was disciplined at various times for fighting with Andrew, disobeying mum or dad, lying and talking back to my parents, who weren't above giving us a smack when we deserved it. Mum and Dad exercised their parental authority in a very balanced way, but they weren't perfect either, and sometimes 'did their block' disproportionately. On the rare occasions when that happened, though, Mum (who had a shorter fuse than Dad) always apologised if injustice had been done on her part. So on these and other occasions, we learnt the importance of saying sorry and not allowing anger to fester.

Mum and Dad lived their faith in tangible ways and modelled to us practical Christianity, always giving of themselves to others. Dad mowed the lawns of elderly people in the church, Mum visited folks who were sick or made an apple pie or a meal for someone who was bereaved or going through a difficult time. She was often seen writing letters or making phone calls to someone who needed encouragement.

Our material blessings were shared too, by giving money to the church and charity or mission organisations. For many years we sponsored children in Africa or Asia through World Vision. My parents were not 'Sunday Christians'. God was involved in every aspect of their lives in a way that seemed perfectly natural. We said grace before meals, were read Bible stories at night before bed, listened to lots of kids' tapes with fun Christian songs, and prayed out loud to God from an early age.

My childhood was generally a very positive experience, but life deals out difficult and unexpected times to everyone, and our family also endured times of stress and trauma. There were tears as well as laughter in our house, but even in those hard times there was a sense, demonstrated through the responses of my parents to these situations, that God loved us, was always there with us and would help us, and these difficult issues were taken to Him in prayer. Mum and Dad showed what it was to trust in God at all times, even though we also went through the natural human responses and emotions when faced with adversity.

Kathryn Kerridge

I was raised with knowledge of the difficult circumstances suffered by Christians in other parts of the world, simply because they had chosen to believe in God. From my parents' 'mission-mindedness', Andrew and I inherited awareness that it wasn't only material poverty from which millions suffered. Not everyone in the world had freedom to express their faith openly, freedom to obtain a Bible, or even the means of finding out more about God if they so desired.

As a child, I heard often the names of Brother Andrew, Richard Wurmbrand, Gladys Aylward (a friend of my maternal grandparents), Corrie Ten Boom, and of organisations such as 'Operation Mobilisation', 'Voice of the Martyrs' and 'Open Doors'. The newsletters of various missionaries and organisations were delivered to our letter box regularly. I grew up knowing that if you were a Christian, God might call you to go to another country to help other people understand more about Him. In fact, we had a number of family friends who either had been, or were at that time ministering in other parts of the world in various capacities.

Sunday was a sacred day in our house. Our priority that day was going to church together, Andrew and I attending Sunday School and Mum and Dad teaching Sunday School classes. Grandma and Grandpop Kerridge came to the same church, as did an aunt and uncle and some cousins. Hearing about God and learning from the Bible seemed completely natural to Andrew and me, although in all honesty, we kids sometimes did find the church sermons rather boring and tedious.

After the service we were free to race around the church grounds with the other kids, getting hot and sweaty as we chased each other and played hide-and-seek. Pungent, ripe (and rotten) bright orange persimmons had to be dodged, but the deliciously sweet and juicy mulberries from the bush in the corner were highly prized. Mum would look suitably horrified at my purple-stained fingers and then to my Sunday best dress to see if her painstakingly-sewed creation was forever ruined with purple splodges. Well, the silkworms residing in the shoebox in my room had to be fed...

The Kerridges were renowned for being the last to arrive at church and the last to leave on a Sunday morning. Actually by the time we drove away it was well into lunchtime, so our suggestion of fish and chips or a pie for lunch was frequently acceded to. That was about the extent of the fast food component of our diet.

There were times during my childhood and teenage years when I approached Sunday with a 'Do we *have* to go to church?' attitude, I must admit, but I found that if for some reason we were unable to go, I felt that something significant had been missed. I could sense somehow the importance of attending church

Kathryn Kerridge

with other believers to learn from the Bible and spend relaxed time together afterwards.

At no time were Andrew and I under any pressure from our parents to become Christians. The relevant information was presented to us but the decision was ours alone. My time came early at five years of age while attending a Vacation Bible School run by my church. I had heard how Jesus died on the cross for me, and I wanted to accept His forgiveness for my sins and follow Him all my life and be His friend. Obviously my childlike understanding of God and what it would mean to commit my life to Him was limited; nevertheless, the commitment was real and my personal relationship with God began that day.

We always had illustrated children's Bibles in the house, but I received my first 'grown-up' Bible for my seventh birthday. The simplest version published at the time was the Good News Bible. Obviously it was still a rather weighty tome for a seven year old, but I was nevertheless able to read and understand familiar Old Testament stories about Noah, Moses, Joseph, Esther, Ruth and others, and the gospels in the New Testament containing accounts of the life of Jesus. Besides, the Good News version had those funny little stick figure pictures to look at, and I remember passing many church sermons that I couldn't understand going through my Bible looking for all those little drawings. Another Sunday morning when I was a few years older, I decided to try to memorise all the books of the Bible. By the time the sermon was over and it was time to sing the last hymn, I could indeed recite the entire list faultlessly. A good memory was another of my gifts.

God had always felt real to me, and a couple of my most vivid childhood memories involve answers to my prayers. On one occasion, when I was about seven or eight years old, I had arrived at school only to discover to my distress that I had left an important project at home. It was due that day, and I was desperate not to get into trouble from my teacher. I don't really remember the mental process I went through, but I clearly remember perching on the little brown fence by the front of the school gate when my mum drove up to the school about two minutes before the final bell rang for the start of class.

When Mum asked me what I was doing there, I replied calmly that I had prayed to God that she would find the project and bring it to me, and I was just waiting for her to come. Utterly astonished at that expression of childlike faith, (as I am now when I think of it), she had certainly not expected to find me by the front gate waiting for her. That little brown fence, a bit dilapidated now, is still standing at my old primary school, just down the road from where my parents live today. Each time I walk by it, I am reminded of the little girl with her hair in pigtails, waiting patiently for God to answer her prayer, utterly convinced that He would.

Kathryn Kerridge

Fast forward a couple of years to find our family relaxing on a week's beach holiday at Burleigh Heads on the Gold Coast. I awoke one night absolutely terrified by a horrible nightmare and was overwhelmed by a tangible and oppressive sense of fear and evil. My body felt paralysed in my bed, and all I could think to do was to whisper the name of Jesus over and over again to myself. After a while, the terror left me and was replaced by an equally tangible sense of God's peace and comfort, and I was able to go back to sleep. I knew that just as the presence of evil was very real, so was the presence of God; that His power was far greater and He was always available for me to call on for help, day or night. He was never asleep or too busy to hear and respond to my prayers.

My primary school years were mostly happy ones. I was blessed with caring and dedicated teachers and no lack of good friends. I worked hard at my school work with great success, but my competence in the sporting arena was, shall we say, rather limited. Although always one of the last few kids to be picked for organised sports teams, I was active in lunch-times playing games with my best friends - marbles, yo-yos, elastics, knucklebones – whatever was the latest craze in the school yard. I was a tomboy who wore shorts under my school dress so I could do handstands and cartwheels with some degree of decency, and a baseball cap was a more or less permanent fixture on my head in Grades 6 and 7, so much so that I often had to be reminded to take it off when we went back into class after lunch.

Being a Christian didn't seem a big deal in those years. I don't remember times of articulating my faith to other kids, but it was known that I went to Sunday School and church. This fact didn't lead to any teasing as probably at least half the children in my class went to Sunday School regardless of whether their parents had any faith commitment; it was just the 'done thing' back then. Besides, there wasn't much else to do on that day – shops and cinemas weren't open, very few people worked, and sports fixtures weren't played on a Sunday.

I certainly didn't feel 'on my own' in my faith. I knew other children at school from Christian families who went to various churches in the district; some of these were close family friends whom I regularly saw outside of school.

At the age of nine, I attended my first week-long 'Winter Warmth' holiday camp. Run by the Presbyterian Church, most years this camp was held at 'Camp Duckadang' in the Brisbane Valley. I loved that place, both for the location and for what was in store for us once we piled off the bus on our arrival. Several things were guaranteed about the week – loads of great singing, fun Bible teaching with drama, puppets and games, leaders whom we looked up to as 'heroes', reunions with old camp friends and the anticipation of making new ones, and absolutely freezing weather. We'd usually wake up in the mornings to see the ground white with frost, with a temperature still only in single figures at breakfast time. (To a suburban Brisbane kid from the mild-weathered bayside, this was REALLY cold – I only ever saw frost on the grass at this camp and if we went to visit relatives in Stanthorpe.) Being a leader on a Winter Warmth camp involved a number of challenges, one of which quite often was making sure your campers were out of bed in time to get dressed and ready for breakfast. One solution to this problem was to upend sleeping bags and tip the sleepyheads out! Yes, I had to be shaken out of my warm cocoon on more than one occasion.

One year 'Winter Warmth' camp was held at an alternative campsite a couple of hours inland from Brisbane, in Toowoomba, which was generally known for freezing winter weather. This site, in contrast to Duckadang, was rickety and old, and it was to one's advantage to be in the front of the shower queue in order to get in before the hot water ran out. I seem to recall only having a couple of showers that week. In the mornings I was so cold I sometimes simply pulled my clothes over the top of my pyjamas. Quite ingenious, I thought – not only did I save time and could stay in bed that bit longer in the mornings, but I didn't have to bare my skin to the nippy winter morning air (no central heating here). Well, it wasn't as if you got hot and sweaty as in summertime, was it? Going to the loo was a bit dodgy at times as a green tree frog used to pop up every now and then in one of the girls' toilets. If a high-pitched scream resounded from a cubicle, you knew to avoid using that one.

Those camps were a key element of the growth of my faith in my upper primary years, and I was so eager to go that my application form was always sent in as soon as the brochure was received. To this day, nearly thirty years on, I can remember the names and faces of many of the leaders, some of the daily Bible verses we memorised for prizes, as well as many of the songs. I was too shy to ever go to camp on my own, though, so always went with a friend, and in my last year (which was actually Grade 8 when I went as an assistant leader) my brother and three of my cousins (from two different families) came along as well. At a couple of meals, we actually had a Kerridge family table!

My biggest traumas at primary school generally fell into one of two categories – friendships and schoolwork. It was devastating if one of my friends decided to 'not talk to me', and it would upset me if any of my friends were fighting with each other. Conflict was very stressful to me and so I would do everything possible to smooth things over and bring about resolution. When harmony was restored, I was at peace again.

In one respect, I was very social with an effervescent and loquacious personality ('talks or giggles too much in class' was frequently heard at parent-teacher interview time), but in situations with strangers, I was painfully shy.

This was quite evident at pre-school, when I apparently managed to attend the whole year hardly saying a word to one of my teachers (although I remember that I adored her). I'm not entirely sure how I managed this feat – it seems an impossibility to me today.

On my first day of primary school, after Mum delivered me to the classroom and then left me to settle in, I promptly went and parked myself under the teacher's desk! There were no tears, but the whole experience was quite overwhelming. Mrs Smith, my teacher, tried to coax me out by craftily depositing a handful of jelly beans on her desk, but I still wouldn't budge until she'd turned her attention to another child. Eventually the lure of the sweets proved too much. How thoroughly disappointing to discover that in the meantime, another child had swiped them off the table.

Academically I flourished at school. Most of my subjects – English, Maths, Science, Social Studies, Art, Music and P.E – easily held my attention. From the beginning, I excelled at my schoolwork, and although I was never pushed by Mum or Dad to attain certain standards, self-motivation propelled me along. Earning great marks resulted in a sense of achievement and satisfaction unmatched by anything else and I became accustomed to being in the top few students in my class every year. For the greatest part of primary school an ongoing and fierce but friendly competition flared with another girl called Kathy for the highest marks in every test and overall top spot. Sometimes Kathy was the victor; sometimes it was me. My perfectionist tendencies were clearly emerging and I became extremely upset with myself (even to the point of tears) if my self-imposed standards and expectations were not attained.

One thing I most certainly did not excel at, however, was P.E. Outside school hours I was very active outdoors with my brother and other neighbourhood children, but when it came to organised sport…well, that was another story. However, perhaps surprisingly, my lack of skill didn't result in a dread of P.E. classes. After all, I had some other less-than-sporty friends, and we could make productive use of the time. For example, playing softball or cricket was a good excuse for us to go stand together near the boundary and have a girly chat, hoping the ball wouldn't come anywhere near us to interrupt! I missed the ball more than I caught it; was accustomed to coming last in running races; and was classified a 'turtle' or a 'stone' during swimming season where the better groups were called 'sharks' and 'fish'. I still remember trying as hard as I could at each activity and besides, I could still ride my bike, play backyard cricket and jump off the ten-metre diving tower at the local pool, giving my brother and cousins a run for their money, and I continued to have a love of the outdoors which kept me active and healthy and balanced out the bookish side of my nature.

A creative bent continued to emerge strongly at primary school. From my imagination appeared written stories which were usually pages longer than everyone else's, and the opportunity for extra Art on a Friday afternoon when the sports teams were playing inter-school matches was relished. Any project for any subject became cause for artistry. Hour upon hour was enjoyably spent decorating cover sheets, borders, posters, and doing illustrations.

Perhaps sensing some musicality in me, Mum enrolled me in piano lessons with our church organist. I loved being able to play completed songs, but found practising and scales tedious so became master of a million excuses to avoid both. Theory was somewhat of a struggle, and I detested my weekly homework. After a couple of years of trying to evade regular practising when I would rather be outside burning off my energy or working on Brownie badges, Mum finally relented and I was allowed to quit. Thus my formal music lessons ended.

My love for music itself continued nonetheless. I unselfconsciously sang along to tapes in the car, joined some eisteddfod choirs at primary school, and picked out tunes by ear on the piano or organ at home. One positive outcome of all those piano lessons was a general understanding of and an ability to read music. In Grades 6 and 7, I learned the kettle drum at school and was part of a small band that 'marched' everyone off parade each week. The drum roll in the middle of 'God Save the Queen' (our then national anthem) was the moment of glory for the kettle drummers!

The end of 1982 heralded the conclusion of my primary school days. A new phase of my life was about to begin, but for this rather shy child the prospect of starting over at high school was not one to which I looked forward with confidence. The butterflies in my stomach were working overtime.

Kathryn Kerridge

Chapter 3

The initial plan for my secondary school education was attendance at one of the large state high schools in my area (there was no 'catchment' area requirement so the choice was ours). However, one of my close primary school friends was booked into a small private girls' school about twenty minutes away from our home. Previously a boarding school, it had been on the verge of closure the decade before but was now operating as a day school only and with much lower fees than the larger, more prestigious Brisbane private schools. My parents' attention was drawn to investigate further, and it was discovered that there were still places remaining for girls to begin Grade 8 (the first year of high school in Queensland) the following year.

So halfway through Grade 7, I found myself sitting in the Moreton Bay College (MBC) headmaster's office with Mum and Dad, being interviewed. The headmaster was a very tall and imposing man and the whole experience was a bit scary for a short eleven-year old girl, but the end result was acceptance into what was to be my high school. I did have my doubts about the strict uniform code at first. For a tomboy who lived in shorts, sneakers and a baseball cap most of the time, the prospect of a uniform which included a panama hat (in summer), a maroon beret (in winter), maroon gloves, and polished black leather school shoes didn't exactly engender great enthusiasm!

I was delighted that I wouldn't be facing this new world alone. Two of my best friends from primary school were coming, as well as another friend from my Brownie pack.

I needn't have worried about making new friends – in the first few months of Grade 8, strong bonds were formed with a group of girls who were truly 'kindred spirits'. They would become, along with the three girls I already knew, my closest friends with whom I would share the agonies and ecstasies of adolescence – exams, boys, bad hair days, 80's fashions and music. We all had similar values and some of the girls were Christians, so I never felt alone or isolated in my faith during those years. Moreton Bay College was a Uniting Church-governed school which held religious assemblies each week, as well as weekly Religious Education classes. There was not necessarily a higher proportion of Christian students or teachers in the school just because it was a church school, but everyone was expected to abide by the spiritual ethos and participate in the spiritual events, whatever personal beliefs one held.

As I continued to mature physically, so my faith continued to grow and deepen. At the age of twelve and within a few months of beginning high school, a situation arose which resulted in my Christian faith becoming very public to the rest of my classmates. I had felt very uncomfortable about an activity that was to form part of several classes in one subject - so much so that I went home and asked Mum to write a note of excusal from that class for reasons of religious belief. A few other Christian girls had done the same, but while I was not standing alone, it was not an entirely comfortable situation. I wasn't embarrassed about being a Christian, but at the same time, I might have been a lot 'quieter' about my faith had I not had to make such a public stand so early on. From that point, it seemed pointless to be shy about my faith, and this probably contributed to a general boldness that was of benefit to me from then on when it came to speaking to others about God.

I did receive some teasing or pointed jibes from some of the other girls at school about my faith in God, but I honestly cannot say that I found it difficult to be a Christian at high school. A bit of cattiness every now and then was all that had to be endured, and God had blessed me with a circle of supportive friends who either shared my beliefs or accepted without fuss my stance.

The commencement of a Scripture Union lunchtime group when I was in Grade 9 was a great encouragement. Two faithful and dedicated ladies came to the school once a week to help lead the group and in my senior year I was involved in that leadership.

Despite the fact that my faith remained of great importance in my life, the consistency of my relationship with God waxed and waned in my teenage years, and I became very slack with my personal Bible reading and prayer at times. However, at no point did I feel inclined to ditch my faith as irrelevant, or because I felt it was too restrictive; neither did I ever question the existence of God, as I had experienced His presence and faithfulness too much to doubt. The deep-down desire of my heart was more than ever to live God's way and follow His will for my life. As my knowledge of the Bible grew and I continued to see His guidance, help and answers to my prayers in all aspects of my life, my faith flourished.

Much credit for this must be attributed to the consistent and faithful example of many older Christian people in my life – parents, grandparents, folks at church and youth group, Sunday school teachers, camp leaders and some of my school teachers as well as my peers as we walked through the Christian life together with all its ups and downs.

High school, as with primary school, was generally a positive experience for me. I continued to excel academically, and thrived on striving to achieve high marks. However, while the end results were laudable, the process involved living under intense amounts of pressure to live up to my high standards. My teachers encouraged and challenged me to reach my potential and there was great emphasis on academic achievement within the private school atmosphere, but I was very much my own slave-driver, berating myself ceaselessly if I failed to achieve perfect or near-perfect results. In fact, it was often left to my parents and teachers to help me come to terms with my perceived 'failures', and to see that doing my best was in fact, good enough. The problem was that if '*my* best' wasn't '*the* best', I could sink into a depression for days. Clearly I couldn't forever live under that kind of pressure, and what I simply thought of as 'excellent and of a high standard' was a sometimes impossible ideal that was actually unreachable. God would certainly have to do some work on this aspect of my nature if it wasn't to ultimately destroy me.

My gifts clearly lay in the arts/humanities stream in subjects such as English, History, Geography and French. It became clear as the years progressed that my brain just didn't 'get' stuff in the maths/physics/chemistry-type realm, regardless of the countless hours I spent on homework or studying. I chose for my senior subjects English, French, Modern History, Geography, Accounting and Maths 1 (alas, we all had to do *one* Maths subject…this one was there to keep me humble, no doubt, and I wrestled mightily with it for the full two years but with limited success).

Extra-curricular activities provided opportunities to balance out the load of study. Not surprisingly I joined choirs for eisteddfods, and was involved in school singing right through from Grades 8 to 12. However, there were a couple of unexpected developments, one being that I actually became 'sporty' - something I never would have predicted from my primary school years.

In Grade 8 P.E. I was introduced to the sport of volleyball, a game very few of us had played before. Developing a real liking for it, I dared to try out for the volleyball teams for the winter inter-school fixtures. To my utter amazement, I won a place in to the C-grade team. In all honesty, this wasn't due to my superior level of skill but rather that most of the very athletic girls played netball, tennis or hockey. In my first year, I rarely made the starting six, but my saving grace was a decent serve through which I usually won some court time in each match.

My love for the game grew and grew and over the years, my ability actually began to correspond with the hours I spent on the court practising. For five years I played for my school, progressing from C-grade to B-grade and then finally to A-grade. I quite literally threw myself into the game, fearlessly diving all over the floor to retrieve the ball, wearing out several pairs of knee-pads during my 'career' in the process.

Volleyball was an activity in which I willingly immersed myself in any spare moment. However, in my senior year I was thrown into another realm of activity that made me feel sick to my stomach with fear every time.

Kathryn Kerridge

By the age of sixteen, the words 'bubbly, lively and loud' were commonly used by others to describe my personality. These were true when I was at school or around my friends, but painful shyness overrode when with groups of people I did not know.

This same paradox applied to public speaking. No nervousness emerged when giving speeches or oral assessment in front of classmates in English or French; in fact, I even enjoyed it. However, even the thought of standing up in front of a crowd of strangers to debate or make speeches would make me feel sick to the stomach for days beforehand. Fear and worry sapped my strength and my sleep.

God knew that conquering this shyness was necessary to fulfil His plans for my life, so in my senior year He arranged for me a position in which public speaking and meeting lots of new people in a variety of contexts was something I would not be able to avoid.

At the beginning of Grade 12, I was elected a School Captain, a House Captain, and the school Volleyball Captain. Proud of MBC, I felt privileged to be chosen for these positions, as well as a bit surprised as I had never considered myself particularly 'popular', or felt very poised or eloquent either. My faith made me determined to be an excellent example of Christian leadership to the staff and students of the school. Little did I suspect some of the challenges that would lie ahead.

From the Ends of the Earth

The Volleyball Captain bit was fine – it certainly wasn't difficult to continue indulging my passion, to train hard and play loads of volleyball. The House Captain bit wasn't too stressful either – some up-front stuff was involved, but I could cope with a school audience. The School Captain position was the biggest challenge, not so much for what it involved within school life, but for the fact that I would have to represent the school on many outside occasions, sometimes just to mingle and chat with other people, sometimes to give speeches at events, and if there was ever an urgent need for a school representative in a public speaking competition…you got it, we captains were right in the firing line. Gulp!

In fact, I was entered into a public speaking competition within weeks of the commencement of my senior year. Sleep was elusive for several nights beforehand – I could barely think of anything else but what lay ahead. Although on competition night I managed to get through the prepared speech section, the impromptu speech was nothing short of a nightmare! It involved walking out onto the stage, reading the current events topic on a piece of paper on the rostrum, and immediately speaking on that topic for two minutes. Two minutes?! I could have sworn I was up there two *hours* before the concluding bell rang. How ironic that the competition was entitled the 'Voice of Youth' because much of the time I spent frozen to the spot, speechless. The feeling of all those people in the audience staring at me while I tried to spit out a few coherent words can still make me cringe. Thank goodness for my trusty friends who spent the following half hour passing encouraging notes to me along the row while all the other confident and eloquent speakers strutted their stuff. I certainly didn't win any prizes for that little outing, and I relived the horror in my mind for several days afterwards.

As the year continued, public speaking to unknown crowds progressed from being terrifying to merely nerve-wracking, and although I never reached the point where it felt natural, I inevitably became accustomed to it. My final oration as a representative of my school was a senior farewell at Speech Night. I don't think I felt very nervous at all, which proves the minor miracle that God had worked in my life over the preceding year.

I really loved high school. Sure, the exam periods were pretty stressful, mostly thanks to the pressure I put on myself rather than my inability to do the work, but there was safety and security in this caring and God-sympathetic environment. I had faithful and fun-loving friends, excellent teachers under whose guidance I thrived, and a plethora of enjoyable activities in which to engage.

However, school doesn't last forever, and about halfway through my senior year, the question had to be faced - what would I do after leaving MBC? Unlike many of my peers, I never had any burning passion for a particular career (not even as a child), and the

From the Ends of the Earth

pressure of choosing what to do next was quite scary. Incredibly, I even considered repeating Grade 12 to provide some extra decision-making time. (That was a merely brief and rather idiotic consideration which ended as soon as I recalled all those assignments and exams which would have to be repeated.)

The time came for us to fill out our tertiary admission forms, reference for which was a weighty tome of all Queensland universities and colleges and the courses each one offered. Our task was to select six preferences in descending order of choice. *Six*? I was struggling to find *one* thing that I could see myself doing as a career. What on earth was I going to do for the rest of my life?! Aaaagh!

Given my academic ability, it was pretty much a given that I would attend university, and indeed I wanted to. The million-dollar question was – to do what?

Our class was allowed an English lesson in which to complete our Queensland Tertiary Admissions Centre (QTAC) form. Frantically leafing through the QTAC book, I waited in vain for something to leap out at me as the answer to my future. God, however much I wanted Him to, didn't reply in a loud voice with the instant solution to my dilemma, and the lesson ended with me seated in front of my still-blank form which would now have to be filled out in my own time and returned in a few days.

Kathryn Kerridge

Obviously sensing my distress, my English teacher, who was also our Director of Studies, came to my rescue and offered to discuss my options. This teacher, who had known me since Grade 8, was a very wise man with a good understanding of my gifts and personality, and calmly and methodically he talked me through my appropriate choices. What a godsend, as I was feeling neither calm nor methodical at the time; clearly God was using the wisdom of this trusted person to help guide my decision.

Any tertiary course requiring prerequisites of maths or science subjects was immediately disregarded, as I hadn't studied those subjects in senior. The only thing I thought I might *like* to do was an Arts degree, as I loved humanities subjects such as History, Geography, French and English. Mr Roberts suggested that since I would easily achieve the required Tertiary Entrance (TE) score for Arts, I should combine that with a Law degree as my first course preference. Gradually a list was compiled of five other courses, which included Business Communications, Social Work and Teaching.

Law? I had never considered becoming a lawyer, and it did seem a daunting sort of career for someone like me who was quite shy and lacked self-confidence, but I would certainly be up for the challenge of the study. Just give me pen and paper and essays and arguments to write, and lots of reading and research – that kind of thing was right up my alley. There

From the Ends of the Earth

were no legal practitioners in my wider family and I didn't really have an extensive idea of what the profession involved.

The question of my future arose again during an English project that year. We were to compile an 'Identity Book', the scope of which was largely up to us in terms of what we included in the way of photos and written pieces, but there was a compulsory piece entitled 'My Views and Philosophy of Life'.

Tackling this assignment with typical artistic gusto, I bought a huge art sketchbook and filled it with decorated pages of writing and photos and lists – from stories of my childhood and family, to a diary of a week in my life, to lists of 'favourites'. My compulsory essay was essentially an exposition of how my faith affected my life. My relationship with and knowledge of God and His Word shaped my views and philosophy of life; I couldn't separate my faith and my life because they were intertwined.

The final two pages of my Identity Book (appropriately decorated with a coloured question mark 'watermark' design) were entitled, 'What of the Future???' I wrote of the possibilities that I felt my future held. Interestingly, although I had no clear vision of what on earth I would do when I finished school, let alone in the long-term, I mentioned the possibility of missionary work in other parts of the world.

Kathryn Kerridge

I can't say what motivated that statement, as I actually wasn't particularly enthralled with the idea of being a missionary. To me that image was very much of remaining a single woman (and I wanted to be married) going to isolated and deprived parts of the world for the rest of my life (and I was quite a homebody). A few other girls in my class spoke of 'going to Europe' or 'backpacking', but that idea didn't grab me at the time at all.

Yet there must have been some sense in my mind that God might well ask me to go somewhere else to work for Him, and if that was the case, I would obey. My mission and desire was follow where He led – that much is crystal clear from the words I wrote back then. That 'missionary' statement would prove to be quite prophetic in fact, but God had a great deal of preparatory work to do on me before I was anywhere *near* ready to go down that path. Little did I know…and actually, I'm glad I didn't, because I'm sure I would have 'done a Jonah' and run in the opposite direction for a very long time.

Grade 12 drew to a close. My hard work was rewarded with a number of awards at Speech Night. I gave my final speech as School Captain, said emotional goodbyes to teachers and school friends, and that was it – twelve years of schooling done! All that remained was to wait for the delivery in the mail of my TE score, when I would find out into which university course I would be offered a place.

From the Ends of the Earth

Beavering away the days of my summer holidays in an office job, time passed slowly but surely until the week before Christmas when the all-important QTAC envelope finally arrived in the mailbox. I opened it to find the second-highest possible TE score and acceptance into a combined Bachelor of Arts/Bachelor of Laws degree at the University of Queensland.

The next phase of my life, five years of full-time university study, was about to begin. I would discover that God had planned it jam-packed with challenges to deepen and challenge my faith still further, and stretch my abilities to the limit. He would also begin to uncover other abilities still buried within under layers of shyness and fear; and everything before me was carefully and lovingly orchestrated for training and preparation in every detail for my life's course in the years to come.

Far more important to God than anything I could *do*, however, was my character, the person I was inside. Sure, there was a lot of good in there – I was friendly and kind, motivated, disciplined, conscientious, helpful, obedient, honest, committed and loyal. But oh boy, there were some destructive 'weeds' that would have to be pulled in order for me to reach the potential that God could see. I was dangerously perfectionist, painfully shy, fearful, stubborn, impatient, competitive and prone to jealousy. I also tended towards people-pleasing to avoid conflict, and was quite insecure, influenced far too much by what other people thought of me. Perseverance was in short supply – if I couldn't pick something up quickly and do it to my high standards first time round, quitting was my instinctive response. I had no patience for doing things over again if I failed the first time. There was a lot of work to be done in me and on me in the years to follow, and the next 'boot camp' was university.

From the Ends of the Earth

Chapter 4

The first challenge to face was moving out of home. Although the University of Queensland (UQ) was only on the other side of Brisbane from where I lived with Mum and Dad, I didn't have a car and the public transport routes meant that I would have to catch a combination of bus, train and/or ferry to get there each day. The journey time would be between one and a half and two hours each way. Dad had a cousin who lived near the campus, and it was arranged that I live with him and his son during the week, and go home on weekends so I could stay in touch with my friends and my church.

Although I was technically living with relatives, they were strangers to me at first. Despite their friendliness and warm welcome, my shyness meant that it took me quite some time to feel 'at home'. Of course there were all the other learning aspects of moving out of home as a teenager, not the least of which was the realisation of just how much Mum had done for me over the years in terms of housework! I had to learn to notice what needed to be done, and then actually do it – it wasn't that I didn't know *how* to cook, wash, iron and clean…it's just that I was realising that there wasn't some household fairy who was going to go around and do things if I didn't! Dad's cousin, Peter, can be heartily congratulated for his great patience with me, especially in those early months.

Starting university was initially an experience in loneliness. Close friends and family had always surrounded me and MBC had been so small when I started Grade 8 that by the time that year was halfway though, I knew the names of almost everyone in the school. Now I was but one on a huge campus of about 25 000 enrolled students, and although five other girls from my Grade 12 class were also commencing degrees at UQ, we were scattered all over the campus in different faculties and wouldn't bump into one another during the normal course of the day. Only one of these girls was a close friend anyway, and while we managed to meet up occasionally in those first weeks, I was largely on my own. Orientation week parties and pub crawls didn't appeal to me as a way of settling in, and I was far too shy to go alone anyway.

And so for those first few painful weeks, I would walk the ten minutes from the house to uni with knots in my stomach, negotiate the maze of lecture theatres and tutorial rooms, and sneak in to sit at the back on my own, hoping to go unnoticed so I wouldn't have to talk much to anyone.

Studying law itself was a challenge – I had no family members or friends in the profession, and the lectures, classes and case law involved learning in a way which was totally new to me. I had been

From the Ends of the Earth

considered 'smart' at school, but here I was with 300 other first-year law students who had all been among the smartest at theirs. Intimidated by the confidence and intelligence of those around me, I felt very out of place, rather like an imposter. I had certainly gone from being a big fish in a small pond, to being a tadpole in a huge lake…at least that was how it felt to me.

All these challenges drew me closer to God than ever before. I was depending on Him for details in my life that I had blithely been able to take care of by myself up until then. Being out of my comfort zone drove me into a deeper relationship with the one Person who remains constant and unchangeable in His love and provision. Rising early each morning, I spent substantial time reading the Bible, praying and listening to Christian music to boost my courage and my spirits, in a much more disciplined way than I often used to do when I sailed more or less smoothly through life at high school.

Although I often felt alone during those first weeks at uni, I knew that God was with me, and His presence was often very tangible. He knew that I needed good friends, and my path began to cross the paths of others with whom I formed some close and very special friendships. In this whole process, God was dealing with the paralysing shyness that prevented my naturally friendly nature to show through, and which inhibited my ability to initiate contact with people I didn't know. This resulted in destructive self-consciousness, making me far more focused on *me* and my own discomfort in social situations, instead of looking outwards towards other people, considering how I could befriend *them*, make *them* feel comfortable, and get to know them.

One day during the first week of lectures, I was wandering down the corridor of the law faculty offices, idly scanning the notices on a huge bulletin board. My eyes honed in on a flyer for a 'Law Christian Fellowship' group (part of the wider Evangelical Students' campus Christian organisation). I decided to attend the following week, figuring that it would have to be a friendly place to spend a lunch hour.

In the room were gathered about a dozen law students from different stages of the course, and as I walked into the room and recognised a few faces from the law library and from my lectures, my spirit lifted with that immediate sense of belonging that comes from meeting other Christians, even though I didn't know them. Everyone was friendly and welcoming, and I knew that from then on I would make this a regular Monday lunch date. It was encouraging to see the other students in the group in different contexts on campus and to be able to stop and chat or just say hello.

As I left the room at the end of that first meeting, I walked down the stairs with a very pretty blonde-haired girl I recognised from some of my first-year classes. I had noticed her walking into lectures in the first few days of uni, mostly because she seemed to have the poise and confidence that I wished I had. She looked as if she belonged exactly there with everybody else – she was probably brilliant, too, I thought – whereas I felt like a fish out of water that didn't fit in. How stunned I was to find out that this 'all together' person was a Christian, too.

From that time on, Cybéle and I sat next to each other in lectures and went along to LCF together each week. We were kindred spirits in so many ways and shared the same deep faith. Our friendship went from strength to strength, even when our course content diverged in later years. For the last couple of years that we were at uni together, we became prayer partners and met for an hour most Friday afternoons by the campus lake to have lunch and pray with and for each other, our families and our friends.

Another key connection was with a couple of girls who were in one of my French classes. These classes were tutorial rather than lecture size and involved lots of interaction as we completed various language exercises in pairs and small groups.

I quickly befriended a couple of first-year girls from another Brisbane girls' school (one of our MBC volleyball rivals, in fact). There were lots of students from this school attending UQ, including about six doing Law, and also a large group of boys from their 'brother' school, some of whom were in my law classes as well. A large group of these boys and girls usually met together under a particular tree during lunch and I was soon invited along to join them whenever I wanted to. They were a great bunch, and it was a godsend to be able to meet so many people in such a relaxed way, and then later meet them in lectures. Funnily enough, one of the girls in this group had played A-grade volleyball for her school at the same time I was playing for MBC- we would have faced each other on the volleyball court several times as fierce rivals during our high school years.

My passion for volleyball was an inroad to another fantastic circle of people, including many overseas students. One day I went to an advertised inter-faculty volleyball match with a couple of law friends, hoping for a hit on the court, and recognised a number of other familiar faces from the law library.

From then on, a group of us gathered at the volleyball courts at lunchtime, and we combined forces with a group of other guys who played representative volleyball, some for the Queensland team. It was brilliant to pit myself against their level of skill, even if I could walk under the net without ducking when it was at regulation male competition level! At only five feet four inches tall, I wasn't exactly intimidating when I played at the net, but I willingly threw myself around the court trying to make contact with their steep spikes and slamming jump serves. Surely it was not an accident that a few of these guys were Christians as well – God was gradually surrounding me with a wonderfully wide circle of friends, both male and female, of all different backgrounds and life perspectives.

I also developed a good group of Christian friends at another Brisbane university, which was attended by one of my close friends from high school. Before I made so many good friends at my own university, I often caught a bus into town to meet her, sometimes attending the CF (Christian Fellowship) lunchtime group. Here I met a fantastic variety of people with whom I would stay in touch in the following years. They, along with the Christian friends I had at UQ, proved vitally encouraging and strengthening to me as we all continued our different journeys of faith.

Over the summer holidays, I experienced my first Scripture Union (SU) Beach Mission, the team of which was predominantly composed of students from this CF group. That experience kicked off an involvement in SU leadership on camps, beach missions, and in other capacities that started in Australia, but later in life led to the other side of the world.

As time passed, I naturally became more comfortable with people, my studies and my new home, and although shyness would still bring butterflies to my stomach at times, God was definitely reducing its impact so that it would no longer inhibit relation-ships with people. Although I had no idea at the time, this was all part of my character-building and training so that God could later send me all around the world on various missions for Him. Travelling alone to foreign countries, meeting lots of new people, and coping with new situations and cultures would become part of my life, but I was nowhere near ready for that yet.

Academically, there were some hard lessons to learn during that first year at university. I had worked hard at school, yes, but I was equally able to rely on an excellent memory and natural ability – the combination of which meant that I was able to get away with a significant amount of procrastination and 'cramming' and yet still achieve excellent results. I wasn't lazy, but I also wasn't very consistent in balancing my workload. After all, our school year was divided into four terms of almost equal length. Most subjects had end-of-term exams for that term's work, and therefore my head usually only had to hold up to eight weeks' worth of study notes at any one time. I would often memorise tens of pages of notes the night or two before an exam, regurgitate it appropriately to answer the test questions, and then be ready for the next subject the next day.

That worked well for me at school, but a rude shock was now in store. The assessment for my three first-year law subjects consisted of one end-of-year exam for each, covering the entire year's work. I had mostly kept up with the required case and article reading, but about a month before the exams I realised that no amount of cramming and memorising was going to deposit all this stuff in my head and keep it there. Besides, studying law was less about memorising the principles and case law and was more about being able to apply them to simulated situations, and no amount of waffling would disguise not knowing how to do that correctly.

A bit of a meltdown from stress ensued at this grave realisation and from then I knuckled down like crazy and spent every night in the law library until it closed at 10.00pm. I'm sure that as I almost became as much of a fixture as the furniture, the library staff nodded knowingly – they had no doubt seen this behaviour before and probably recognised 'the look'...bags under the eyes, utter exhaustion written all over my face, body stooped under a load of books and folders. I was deeply grateful that I lived so close to the campus. My prayers were more fervent than ever, that God would enable me to come to grips with all the work, and then I promised Him and myself that if I could just get through and pass everything this year, some serious changes to my study patterns would ensue. I really couldn't bear the thought of failing any of my subjects and having to repeat them the next year; I had never failed an exam in my life and the thought did not sit well at all.

A couple of months later, and it was all over. I had faced and survived those huge three and a half hour long, 100% exams (talk about all your eggs being in one basket!) for each of my law subjects. To my tremendous relief I passed them all in addition to doing well in my Arts subjects for both semesters. I moved back home with Mum and Dad for my three months of summer vacation. Completely exhausted, mentally and physically, I didn't take a job over the holidays. All I wanted to do was relax, de-stress, and let my body bounce back to normal.

That summer I was completely wiped out, often sleeping for hours in the afternoons. My conclusion was that it was due to all the stresses of my first year living out of home and dealing with the heavy study workload, but despite all the rest I was giving my body, the situation didn't improve as I expected it should. The weeks went by and I still felt not quite 100% when it was time to go back to uni for second year. Still, I couldn't put my finger on anything in particular that was wrong so I kept living life as normal.

Settling back into uni life didn't take long, even after three months off. I felt like I knew what I was doing this time round in terms of lifestyle and study, and there were lots of familiar faces to greet in lectures and around the library and campus. What a contrast to this point in the previous year! I felt like a different person. It was much easier to settle into a study routine, to make friends of strangers in my new classes and to be involved with social activities and clubs.

I jumped straight back into volleyball, and this time our regular group formed two teams for the lunchtime social competition. There were too many of us for only one team and friends though we were, there were some very fierce matches when our teams vied against each other, especially when we met in the final. It's probably best not to reveal how many afternoon lectures I skipped in second year to stay after lunch on the volleyball courts. True, I had developed a much more consistent pattern of study and it was a positive thing that I was less stressed and perfection-seeking, having come to grips with the fact that no matter how much I worked, I was not destined to become one of the decade's great legal minds. However, I still had a bit to learn about striking the balance between work and leisure.

I was fit, I was active and I loved the outdoors. I caught the odd cold in winter, but otherwise was not sick often. I was eating healthily and had eliminated lots of the junk food and chocolate I once was renowned for consuming. Walking to and from the campus each day, climbing up and down several flights of library stairs and playing as much volleyball as possible kept my body active and fit. I wasn't into partying, went to bed at a decent hour, and was definitely less of a 'stress-head' than I had been at school. My social life was thriving, as was my spiritual life. There was no logical reason that I should be feeling anything but fully alive and well, but there was something not quite right; in fact, it felt as if I was moving in slow motion some days, I was so tired. No, not just tired, but utterly bone-weary and exhausted to the very depth of my being.

Kathryn Kerridge

The only thing I could think of as a cause was glandular fever, so I asked my doctor for a blood test, which came back negative for the virus. No medical problem was found; my conclusion was that I must be just silly or getting lazy, slowing down for no reason. With my driven nature and work ethic, lazy was not a word that was ever ascribed to me and my solution in the absence of any concrete evidence to the contrary was to push myself to do what I had already been doing.....plus some more.

I put it all down to the life of a busy student. After all, I was studying a combined degree full-time, living out of home, playing sport, involved with a couple of Christian groups on campus, going home on weekends to be with friends, going to a church home group on Friday nights, attending youth group on Saturday nights and church on Sundays. Of course I would get tired and anyway, with lectures and tutorials at times varying from 8.00am to 8.00pm, I could easily nip home for a quick nap in the afternoons, adjusting my study timetable accordingly. So that's exactly what I did. Student life was renowned for being a bit erratic anyway, wasn't it?

Third year came and went, and at the end of 1990 I completed my Arts degree with a major in French. As a bit of relief from the intense content of my Law subjects, I mostly selected my Arts subjects for personal interest and as well as French, I enjoyed semesters of American History, Australian History,

From the Ends of the Earth

and Geography. I declined the invitation to put my Law degree on hold for a year and study an Honours year of French. Much as I enjoyed the language, I didn't feel that I would use it as a profession, and would instead complete my Law degree in the next two years as originally planned.

After graduating from Arts, my final two years at uni were composed solely of law studies. A bit of a love/hate relationship with Law was with me right through the course. I never doubted that I was walking in God's will being there, with many encouragements and confirmations to affirm this, but becoming a lawyer still didn't seem to fit who I was in terms of my gifts and passions.

My most enjoyable subjects were 'people-oriented', such as Criminal Law and Family Law; enthusiasm couldn't be mustered for subjects such as Taxation Law, Company Law or Commercial Law, and I certainly couldn't see myself practising them in a legal firm.

Along with a number of good friends from the church youth group I was then attending, I had spent a couple of years volunteering on a Drug-ARM (Drug Awareness and Relief Movement) 'Street Van Team', one of the ministries supported by the church. From 8.00pm on a Friday night until the early hours of the next morning, a team drove around specific suburbs in a specially-marked van. Making contact with groups of young people hanging out on the

Kathryn Kerridge

streets, we distributed hot chocolate, tea, coffee and biscuits, and chatted with them. Our prime motive wasn't evangelism but friendship, although we were often asked questions about God when some of the teenagers discovered that we weren't being paid to be there. Some found it difficult to believe we would give up our Friday nights to befriend and help them because we cared for them as a practical outworking of our faith in God.

Many of these young people were not attending school regularly, came from fractured or dysfunctional families, were in frequent trouble with the police and were abusing drugs and alcohol. My eyes were being opened to a whole shocking world outside the loving, caring and sheltered environment in which I was raised. I found the experience a little scary and quite uncomfortable at first, but soon could see past tough and offhand exteriors to the hurting and wounded hearts underneath that were desperate for love, purpose, acceptance, and relief from the pain of some of the difficult circumstances either dealt to them by life or of their own making.

I wondered if God might be intending to use my Law degree in the area of juvenile justice, perhaps with Legal Aid, representing young offenders. That would definitely be a 'people-oriented' aspect of the law, albeit not a comfortable, cosy or easy one.

The idea appealed to me, and to explore this avenue further, I organised some work experience with the

Juvenile Aid Bureau, a specialised branch of the Queensland Police Force. During that week, I observed the flip side of this legal coin. Accompanying police officers as they conducted interviews with young offenders, we visited detention centres and the Brisbane watch-house and made appearances in court. In addition, some time was spent with the Child Abuse Unit, which I found very harrowing. Not to my surprise I discovered that the turnover rate of staff in this area was very high, particularly among female officers. Much as I loved children and desired to help them, I knew that I would never survive that kind of job – how could I detach myself from the horror stories I would hear and see on a regular basis?

Family Law was another career consideration. Although marriage breakdowns, custody battles and property disputes would be far from clear-cut or easy, I was drawn particularly to the idea of being an advocate for children in such situations.

As my brain was pondering these notions, and as I was trying to understand where this degree was heading in terms of my future, time moved relentlessly on. Fourth year finished, and I soon found myself a couple of months into my final year, sending out resume after resume in search of an Articled Clerkship (a two-year apprenticeship with a law firm, upon completion of which I was eligible to be admitted as a solicitor in Queensland) to commence the following year.

Kathryn Kerridge

Still following my 'people-law' ideas, I targeted firms that included Family or Criminal Law in their practices. I accepted a job with a small Brisbane law firm in which a husband and wife were the partners, and were also Christians. They had a small staff, which also suited me, and my training there would provide a taste of many areas of law, as they did 'a bit of everything'.

Phew! By this stage, it was about May 1992, and it was great to have a job sorted out so early in the year. That was a major stress lifted from my mind. Now all I had to do was focus on my final subjects and make the most of my last year of student life before I could no longer work to my own timetable, sleep when I wanted, and enjoy more than four weeks of holidays each year.

Life was cruising along fairly smoothly. I was doing well in my studies, heading for second-class honours if I could keep my grade point average up. I had blossomed socially in the previous few years, with so much confidence I was now making friends easily in new situations. Emotionally, I had learned to temper my perfectionism and competitiveness, wisely realising that constant comparison with my own impossible standards and the achievements of others was a downhill slide to dissatisfaction and depression. There was still a way to go to deal well with stress, but I had learned to strike a fairly good balance between work, rest and play. Spiritually, I had progressed in leaps and bounds. Having gained a greater dependence upon God through all of the new and difficult experiences I had faced, I had become more involved with ministry opportunities – on campus, at church and youth group and with Scripture Union, taking leadership roles in many of them. My knowledge of God and the Bible had deepened markedly through regular study of His Word.

My faith was as real and relevant as it had ever been, and I found it easy and exciting to share that faith with others when the opportunity arose. Everyone in my friendship circles at uni knew where I stood with respect to God, and many of them would ask challenging questions of me, or would genuinely seek my opinion on different life situations, movies, and moral questions. I relished the way this forced me to think long and deeply about faith issues, and although I didn't always have the answers, I was able to accept that although I myself couldn't understand or explain everything about God or the Bible, that didn't mean either were not worthy of my trust. Some very intellectual and scientific arguments arose with respect to God, and although feeling out of my depth in some of them, nothing I heard rattled me enough to make me question my faith or to consider it suitably undermined for me to discard it altogether.

During my uni years, I had also started travelling. I applied for my first passport in 1989 in preparation for a family holiday to Singapore in early 1990. A

Kathryn Kerridge

Singaporean family from our church was travelling there for a week on business and to visit family and invited us along. Although accommodated in a hotel, most of our time was spent with these friends and other local people.

A key reason for our visit was to enable Grandma Kerridge to visit the Changi Prison site and the Kranji War memorial. Grandpop had passed away on June 30, 1989, after a long battle with cancer and since then, Grandma had been reading and transcribing his war diaries which detailed his experiences and suffering. This would be her opportunity to stand in the place where he was imprisoned as a POW for so many years when she didn't know whether he was alive or dead. It was a very emotional time for her and also for my dad, who would have grown up fatherless had Grandpop not survived.

There was no way to know that Grandma, who was still fit and active, would be killed in a car accident about eighteen months later, so the timing of this visit was certainly a gracious gift of God to our family.

In fact, all four of my grandparents passed away within about four years, during the time I was at university. I hadn't spent much time with my mother's parents during my lifetime, as they lived so far away. It was a twenty-four hour drive from Brisbane to Echuca (where they first lived) and then to Bendigo (where they lived in retirement) in Victoria. Every four years or so, the car would be packed chock-full and we would drive down to see them. My aunt, uncle and cousins from Perth crossed the Nullabor Plain (a twenty-four hour journey west-to-east across this vast continent) to meet us there. Mum's sister and her family and another brother lived in Victoria relatively near my grandparents, and the other brother and his family lived outside Sydney, so we would call in and visit them on the way there or back.

Despite spending little time in their presence, Grandma and Grandpa Frencham made a very definite impact on my life. Grandma and I had been regular pen pals since my childhood – I had clearly inherited my mum's penchant for writing letters – and in her letters, Grandma was always pointing me to Jesus in the everyday things of life, urging me to keep reading my Bible and growing to love and trust Him more. Mum had a small collection of China mementoes – some little wooden toys, and a tiny red silk slipper (smaller than the baby slipper made for my uncle Rob), the size worn by Chinese women forced to have their feet broken and bound from birth. I also heard stories of China and their later life in England from Mum, and her parents to me represented people who loved God and were prepared to suffer hardship for the sake of obeying His call to a far-away country.

Kathryn Kerridge

My immediate and extended family remained an important part of my life as I moved from my teens into my twenties, despite the inevitable transitions as cousins grew up and scattered.

My other overseas experience during those uni years was a trip to Fiji. One of my Street Van/home group/youth group friends had been to Fiji on a number of short-term mission trips, and eventually married the pastor of a church there. I was a bridesmaid for her wedding in Brisbane, and about a year later organised to go and stay with her in Lautoka for two weeks.

For me, it was a holiday and a visit to friends – there was nothing structured within the trip for me ministry-wise, but looking back, I can see God used the time to open my eyes and give me some experience in cross-cultural mission work.

During the two weeks, I learned to accept cold water showers, do all my washing by hand, be aware of dressing and behaving in a culturally appropriate way, eat Indian food traditionally with my right hand and deal with the laid-back 'Fiji time' and way of doing things. I tasted foods I had never seen before and was blessed by the incredible generosity and hospitality of people, most of whom had nowhere near the material possessions that I had.

I lived as the locals did and learned from my friend as she described some of the frustrations and challenges of living in a different culture. However, God had given her a love for Fiji, a calling to go there in the first place, and a wonderful husband with whom to minister. Not the least of the lessons was to be much more thankful for what I had materially, and I felt a renewed sense of responsibility to share it with those who lacked. I had no idea at the time that this was God's gentle introduction to my later destiny in life, when my passport would become a very frequently-used document.

Despite all these years of positive growth and change, there was one aspect of my life that had deteriorated markedly. Despite all health and fitness efforts, my energy levels had continued to decline year by year until they were now so low that I had to literally grit my teeth and will my weary body around from place to place. I was so crushingly tired all the time, no matter the amount of sleep or rest. Muscles, especially in my legs, felt like lead weights and ached constantly, and my concentration and memory seemed to be eroding away to nothing.

Each year since the summer holidays of my first year of uni, I had felt a little worse. Each year I requested a blood test for glandular fever or anything else that could be the cause; each time the results showed all tests were fine and I was in the clear. I should have been relieved, but instead grew only more discouraged that I could be 'perfectly fine' and yet feel so physically awful. How could I justify taking six months off to rest? How could I explain that to people when apparently nothing was wrong?

Instead, I could only conclude that laziness was my problem and that I was just slacking off. The obvious cure was to get a grip on myself, be more self-disciplined, do more and work harder. I cringe when I recall how relentlessly I pushed my body when it was literally screaming out for rest and respite, trying to cope with an illness I didn't know I had. How could I know that I was damaging my body more and more when at the time I was simply trying to keep myself functioning, but barely succeeding?

The constant fatigue, achiness and pain were maddening, as in all other respects, I was having the time of my life. Sure, I can't say I actually enjoyed *all* my studies, but the mental challenge was giving my able brain a workout, I was involved in activities that I loved, had a wide circle of friends, and a job waiting for me next year. It was just such a nuisance to fight through this exhaustion every moment of every day, day after relentless day. Still, at least home was close enough for naps between lectures if necessary, and besides, plenty of people were seen snoozing in the Law Library from time to time. 'Making it work' became my goal, and no one else needed to know how much I actually had to stop to rest and sleep. It was all a bit embarrassing really – no one else seemed to need this much rest – so I said nothing to anyone, not even my family. In public, I

From the Ends of the Earth

kept the smile on my face, the volleyball trainers on my feet, and just plodded on.

By my final year at uni, my life was about as full as it could be. The weekdays were filled with a full course load, three part-time jobs on campus (research assistant to one of my lecturers, night shelver in the Law Library once a week, and social volleyball competition referee), and involvement in Christian groups. Weekends were composed of study, friends, home group, Street Van, youth group and church.

The outward appearance was dangerously deceptive - all was most certainly not well and my body began to break down more noticeably. By the beginning of 'Swot-Vac' study week prior to first semester exams, I was completely and utterly shattered. I went home to Wellington Point for the week, able to manage only two or three hours of study in the mornings before I had to crawl back to bed for the rest of the day. I could manage very little or nothing at night either. Falling very quickly behind my carefully worked study timetable, I felt sick with fear that I would not be able to pass my exams. Despite the work I had done all semester long, there was a lot of material left to memorise, and I was rapidly running out of time. My goal of graduating with second-class honours was slipping through my fingers like water. Now I would be content just to pass everything so I could finish the degree and not have to repeat any subjects the following year.

Kathryn Kerridge

During the exam period, I drove from Wellington Point to uni for each exam with my stomach knotted in fear, praying fervently that God would enable me to pass each subject despite the paltry amount of study I had managed. Gathering outside the exam rooms with other students who had been studying around twelve hours a day, internally I shrank still further as I heard them revising material in those final moments before the tests. What a nightmare! What was going on with my body and brain, neither of which had failed me so greatly before in my life? How *could* there be 'nothing wrong'? This was more than just laziness; it *had* to be.

The struggle continued throughout second semester, my body pushed to its limit. God in His mercy replied to my cries for help with an abundant outpouring of His grace. I received some of the highest grades of my whole degree in that final year of study, and I have no other explanation except that God graciously took account of what I had been able to do and enabled me to sufficiently apply it to my exam and assignment questions. I was getting physically weaker but He was more than able to overrule and compensate with His power. I indeed finished the course with second-class honours. I would officially graduate with my Bachelor of Laws on completion of a few pass/fail 'professional' subjects during my articles the following year.

What a profound relief to be on holidays again, although I only had about five weeks prior to

From the Ends of the Earth

commencing my new job in January 1993. I intended to rest and relax a lot in preparation. The articled clerkship would involve long hours and a fair bit of stress, and I fretted that I was not up to the task. However, I believed that God had clearly revealed this path as the way forward from university, so on I walked.

With a lovely office in my new firm, I was blessed to be working with helpful and kind solicitors and support staff. Boy, did I have a lot to learn, though, and it was difficult not to feel overwhelmed at times with the sheer responsibility of what was before me. Clients were being billed for my time and I needed to be accountable for all the minutes in my day as, by and large, someone was paying for them. The pressure was on as a lack of accuracy or efficiency could cost either the client or the firm a lot of money.

My parents' Wellington Point home was my home again now, and travel time to work in Brisbane city was almost an hour each way by train. Working ten-hour days on average, my body didn't take long to crumble. Gone was the flexibility to choose my own hours or take extra rest. Only two weeks into the job I was in the local hospital on a drip with ear infections in both ears. I felt that I was letting my employers down, and certainly didn't enjoy the pain I was in, but also felt incredible physical relief at being confined to bed to rest. There really had to be something wrong for a hospital stay to feel so positive. Guilt plagued me about this sensation, too. Was I a hypochondriac or very lazy?

Back at work I pressed on learning the practice of law. In addition to working through conveyancing files, I accompanied a solicitor on some Legal Aid work and to a Family Law conference between the parties in a settlement dispute. Although still leaning towards specialising in those types of law, I was experiencing first-hand how harrowing and emotional the reality would be.

Weeks went by, and my body slipped further into decline. Now I could barely get out of bed in the morning, and by the time I had dressed for work, I felt completely spent, ready to crawl back under the covers. However, still with no medical diagnosis, I gritted my teeth and willed myself to walk to the train station, closed my eyes for the hour-long journey, and forced my feet to step off the train and trudge across the road to the office, concentrating mightily on putting one foot in front of the other so I wouldn't simply collapse in a heap on the pavement. Desperately tired, I was close to tears most of the time, wondering how much longer I could possibly continue, but feeling that I could not stop working without a legitimate reason.

I had already withdrawn from the professional subject I was enrolled in at uni. Going to a lecture one evening a week on top of work was too much, so graduation would have to wait a little longer.

From the Ends of the Earth

My brain was starting to break down to the point where I was sometimes simply unable to process information. Physical tiredness was one thing, but when I couldn't make sense of the words on a page, I was even more scared. My brain had always been quick, reliable, able to read and comprehend well, and able to memorise pages of information. I *had* to be able to think and reason in this job. I certainly didn't relish the thought of making any costly errors.

On one occasion I was in the firm's small conference room/library, seated alone at the table, surrounded by legislation and legal texts in order to research an issue for one of the partners. I had just returned from meeting mum for lunch in town.

As I struggled to sift through this mass of information, there was a tap at the door. It was mum again – she'd forgotten to give me something, and had just popped in before going home. Noticing the stricken look on my face, she asked me what was wrong. Fighting back tears, I whispered that I was reading this information, but was unable to understand the words I was reading. This was different from not comprehending some new legal information I had never come across before; this was more like my eyes seeing words that my brain couldn't unscramble and make sense of at all.

For years, I had been able to keep a lid on the true state of my health, but now I was barely holding it together. I knew I couldn't go on much longer. What was I supposed to do? I had tried again with different doctors to get a diagnosis, to no avail. Another battery of blood tests for glandular fever, thyroid function, iron levels etc, etc, etc had all come back clear; I had also been to see a homeopath who diagnosed stress, gave me some products to take and told me to take a couple of weeks off work. He was right – I *was* stressed, but that was not the whole story, I was sure of it. There was something much deeper going on; something was very wrong and was slipping through the net of diagnoses.

By this stage, the symptoms I suffered daily went far beyond bone-numbing fatigue – 'tired' doesn't even begin to describe what I was suffering; 'exhausted' doesn't even do the job. It was as if a vacuum cleaner hose had been attached to my body and had sucked every ounce of energy from me. I had pain in my muscles, joints and bones – it even hurt to touch my skin at times; a sore throat and swollen glands; constantly cold hands and feet; difficulty in concentrating and processing information (as if my brain was 'short-circuiting' all the time); a foggy head that felt full of cotton wool. I couldn't think clearly, finish sentences I'd started, or find the right word for a particular occasion. My eyes were sensitive to light and my ears were increasingly sensitive to noise. My sleep was broken and restless despite the fatigue that made me want to sleep non-stop for months on end.

At the beginning of April resignation was inevitable, diagnosis or not, before I simply collapsed. Feeling helpless and a bit foolish, I sat in my boss' office to try to explain, and I was so grateful for the compassion I was shown. In an effort to understand how ill I was, my boss asked me to imagine myself as an eight-cylinder car, and then asked on how many cylinders I thought I was running. When I said 'a half', his eyes widened – 'What? A half of eight?' When I replied that I meant no, a half of *one* cylinder, he nearly fell off his chair!

He could see that I wasn't simply being melodramatic – there was no energy for that – and agreed that I would need to resign. I would remain until the end of the month to finish up or hand over the client files I was working on, and then I would be released from my contract. It was awful to feel I had let them down, but nothing could be done except to work to my utmost for the next four weeks. After that, who knew what would happen? The future that had looked so promising was now one big question mark. Actually, I didn't even care. What was the future worth when I couldn't even get through one day? My life was being turned completely upside down and it would never be the same again.

Living with my parents meant that my condition could not be hidden from them. It was painfully obvious how much my health had been declining, and they were increasingly worried. Because of their love and concern, there was no pressure for me to continue working from a financial point of view –

they only wanted to see their old daughter back and would do whatever it took for that to happen.

After leaving the law firm, my body went into 'crash mode' and, although I dressed every morning, I didn't spend too much time out of my bed. What I really needed was a diagnosis as it was difficult to explain to people why I had quit work and wasn't doing anything. It was also difficult psychologically for a former high-achiever to be doing nothing without an explanation or excuse, and I fought a daily battle against feeling lazy, worthless and a hypochondriac. I *knew* there was something not right with my body; I *knew* this was not all in my head…why couldn't someone figure out what was wrong?

Perhaps this was the onset of mental illness. One of my grandmothers suffered from depression at one point and an uncle on the other side of the family had schizophrenia. Was I going down that road too? My brain was telling me one thing; my body another. My life felt like an endless waking nightmare.

Doctors had no answers. I visited various GPs for a second, third and fourth opinion, went to a specialist for heart tests, and to a naturopath who diagnosed a few food allergies. I was referred to psychiatrists for suspected depression and had brain scans to check for tumours. I had blood test after blood test, spent dollar upon dollar on naturopathic and homeopathic remedies and swallowed vitamin after vitamin. I was desperate. Still there were no real answers. Nothing I tried was working.

My mind was cast back to a conversation of some time ago with an old high school friend, who also happened to be a Christian. We had lost contact after school, but I had heard that she had to drop out of her university course after only six months due to a viral illness, and had not since been able to either resume her studies or hold down a job.

It seemed that no one really knew what was wrong with her, and I remember feeling puzzled that someone could be so sick and yet not have any concrete explanation. She was finally diagnosed with Myalgic Encephalomyelitis (ME), the recently-coined medical term for what had been known until then mostly as 'Chronic Fatigue Syndrome' (CFS), and colloquially as 'yuppie flu' – because it seemed to hit mostly young professionals and high achievers in their early twenties. The latter felt like quite a disparaging term, making light of the extreme fatigue and pain of the sufferer, and suggesting nothing particularly serious or long-lasting.

At the time, the medical profession, and society in general, held a fairly sceptical attitude towards this 'illness'. Sufferers were quite often seen as hypochondriacs or malingerers, and sympathy was scarce.

A high school 'Old Girls' function afforded the chance to ask my friend more about her illness, symptoms and treatment. The more I heard her describe the past several years of her life, the more I became convinced that my debilitation and numbing fatigue was the same thing. The problem was trying to get a doctor to give me a diagnosis other than that there was nothing wrong with me or that it was stress, or psychosomatic.

My friend gave me the name of a doctor in the city who specialised in the diagnosis and treatment of ME, and I phoned to make an appointment, only to be told there was a six-month waiting list. My heart sank, but with nowhere else to turn, I took the earliest possible appointment.

Weeks of bed rest turned into months. Still without a diagnosis I was not improving as a result of all the rest. This played havoc with me psychologically. It was devastating to have no answer for people who asked the question of why I had left work, and what was wrong with me. That I could only say I didn't know, but I was so tired and weak that I could hardly raise myself from my bed brought sceptical looks to faces, and I knew that some people thought that I was malingering. I had to admit that I probably would have drawn the same conclusion.

I wanted to scream at people – 'Come on, don't you *know* me? I'm *not* lazy. I'm *not* afraid of hard work. I'm *not* a hypochondriac. I love life! How could you think I'm making this up for attention?' In my opinion, you'd be mad to try to fake this illness for attention. It didn't provoke much sympathy, mostly just cynicism and disbelief.

The other mental battle was in trying to rest as my body demanded but, seemingly, with no legitimate reason to do so. I had never been unproductive in my life, and it seemed sheer sloth not to do anything with each day's twenty-four hours when I had no excuse not to. My dad was a farmer who laboured hard twelve hours a day, six days a week to provide for us and put me through university, and yet here I was lying around in my bed all day.

The pendulum swung between being unable to move and forced to do nothing, and garnering some energy to at least crochet a square for a rug, write some letters, or do some craft. It wasn't much, but it gave me the illusion of not being a total sluggard. Of course, I was actually pushing my body further into exhaustion, draining it of any energy salvaged through times of rest.

Thoughtless comments from others hurt deeply. Jibes such as, 'Well, everyone gets a bit tired, you know', 'or 'Couldn't you cope with life in the real world?' and well-meaning questions like, 'Are you *sure* it's not psychosomatic?' all took their toll. Worst of all was the comment one day from a Christian from my church who asked, 'Why did you give up your job? Where is your faith?' 'Just pray and claim your healing' was the glib solution.

Kathryn Kerridge

Where was my faith, indeed? Was my problem a lack of faith that God could heal me, or was there some undealt-with sin in my life that was the cause of this sickness? I began to read through the book of Job with such empathy and understanding that I would weep many times over these pages in my Bible. From the devastation of Job's life and health to the unhelpful judgments and opinions of his 'friends' to his struggles and questions about where God was in all of this – what a relief to read these chapters that spoke so directly to my pain.

In all my life, I had never felt so alone and distant from the God I had loved and followed practically all my life. On top of the physical discomfort and the breakdown of my body, I felt that my heart was breaking too. What about all my hopes, plans, dreams for the future? I was desperately crying out, 'God, where *are* You?'; 'God, do You even *care*?'

I felt like I was losing my grip on my faith and my life, falling endlessly down a cliff, battered and smashed against the rocks as I desperately, and in vain, tried to grab for hand holds. I felt like I was a thin and worn out rag put through endless cycles of a washing machine and dryer until I was sure there would soon be nothing left of me. I felt like I had been run over a hundred times by a steamroller – completely flattened physically, mentally, emotionally and spiritually – and yet it kept turning around and coming back at me again and again.

From the Ends of the Earth

Where would it end? Where was God in it all? Was this to be my life forever…stuck in a bed, useless to anyone, even to Him who was the centre of my life, my purpose for being, for whom I had wanted to live and whom I wanted to serve more than anything else in the world?

Like Job, I asked questions like *'Why didn't I die as I came from the womb?' (Job 3:11 NLT)* - after all, I just about did; *'Why is life given to those with no future, those God has surrounded by difficulties?' (Job 3:23 NLT)*; *'Show me what I have done wrong' (Job 6:24 NLT)*.

I knew in my head that the Bible doesn't promise that Christians won't suffer; in fact, the opposite is true. I knew in my head that just because God allows evil to touch my life, this doesn't mean He is any less God and all-powerful, nor does it mean He cares for me any less as His child. I knew of God's promises of faithfulness and love and care and that He was sovereign and didn't merely exist to eliminate all my discomfort in life; I knew that just because it didn't *feel* like He was close by, that didn't mean He wasn't. Blah, blah, blah – there was an awful lot of Biblical truth in my head, but at this nadir of my life, in utter despair and desperate for some glimmer of hope, I still called out 'Why?' and 'Where are You?'

God was still working with compassion in my life, although I couldn't see it. He saw every tear I cried and felt all the heartbreak and anguish of my body, mind, and soul. He was deeply concerned with my life and was not merely watching dispassionately from afar. But He was far more interested in my growth and strengthening *through* pain than He was with removing it because I didn't like it. God did not enjoy or desire in any way that I suffer with this illness, but He was going to bring His purposes out of this in His way and in His timing.

Of course, that was not what I wanted to hear at the time, either from Him or from anybody else. I was far too raw. To hear someone say not to worry and that God was in control and would work all things together for good was like salt rubbed in a deep wound, and intensely painful. A lot more time would have to pass until I came to that point of acceptance. For the moment, I was simply engulfed in too much hurt and grief to cope with that reasoning, despite the truth in it.

I was grieving the loss of my life as I knew it, the loss of my health, and the loss of my future, and part of my grieving process included wrestling with my faith and my understanding of who God was.

Finally, a crucial breakthrough came in the form of a diagnosis, almost three months after I had to quit my job.

A friend of Mum had heard of a doctor on the other side of the city diagnosing patients who were 'just like me', and we made an appointment to see her as soon as possible. Dad took the day off work to drive us to the surgery an hour away. After sitting in a waiting room full of other exhausted patients who looked just like I felt (i.e. pale, exhausted, washed-out, floppy rag dolls), I was soon sitting in the doctor's office relating my symptoms.

On a return visit, a number of probing questions and blood tests later, I was diagnosed with ME/CFS/Post-viral Fatigue Syndrome (this still relatively unrecognised illness went by a number of names). I almost wept on the spot with the relief of knowing that what I was suffering was real; this was not all in my head, nor was I mentally ill; that there was a physical reason for my appalling state of health, and I was not just lazy.

I was staggered when the doctor pinpointed the start of it all to a bout of glandular fever, hepatitis and another virus dating back about four years. I just *knew* that she was right – I recalled the end of my first year at uni when inordinate amounts of time were spent sleeping through the three-month summer vacation. My body had been thrashed by the viruses and further thrown into turmoil as I had subsequently pushed it to live a normal life in its severely weakened state.

Trying to absorb this information, I was further stunned when the doctor started accurately describing what she imagined my life had been like since then – the range of symptoms I had experienced on a daily basis, the techniques I had been using to cope with the fatigue and pain and to hide it from others, the mental and physical 'pushing' I had been doing to keep going, the psychological toll it had taken.

Unbelievable! This woman didn't know me from a bar of soap, yet she was describing the past four years of my life almost to the letter. In fact, I had been running on adrenalin and stress for so many years just to keep functioning, she estimated I was perilously close to adrenal exhaustion and hospitalisation. I had indeed received this diagnosis just in time. If I'd had to wait another few months for the other doctor's appointment, who knows in what state I would have been?

The doctor's instructions were blunt and non-negotiable from her point of view – if I was to regain any semblance of life and health, I was to go to bed for total rest, do absolutely nothing, and stay there until she instructed me otherwise. The only exceptions to this were to be my fortnightly appointments with her. If I wasn't prepared to follow her orders and treatment, I shouldn't bother coming back! (Her bedside manner was a little lacking, it has to be said, but at this point I would have done *anything* if there was any hope of improvement.)

To help ease my symptoms, I was prescribed twice-weekly vitamin injections along with other medications and vitamins. These included anti-depressants to try to induce some sort of regular sleep pattern, to slow my body down and to stop the flow of adrenalin that my body had been using as its main energy source, as well as to treat some of the symptoms of depression that I was suffering as a consequence of the illness.

So on went my pyjamas and I went to bed. There was an incredible sense of relief to finally have a diagnosis, and not feel that I *had* to be doing something productive with my days.

Not only had God engineered circumstances for this diagnosis and treatment, He also had organised for two wonderful and compassionate nurses to administer my weekly injections. Mum was a nurse prior to my birth, but felt way too rusty to give me shots after twenty years; and there was no way that I was going to let my brother, a student nurse, practise his needle technique on me (much as he begged to be allowed to do so). Twice a week I was visited by a community home-nurse; one on Mondays and another on Thursdays. Both were friendly with a wonderful bedside manner and great gentleness as they delivered these quite painful jabs into my backside. Their visits became a rare bright spot in my week, and it was surely no accident that one of these women was a Christian. She delivered no trite platitudes about God, nor did Bible verses trip lightly off her tongue, nor did she judge – she was just *there* as a nurse and a friend who was trying to help and support me through my pain.

Diagnosis brought financial relief as well. I had been incapable of earning an income for the previous three months, and yet without a diagnosis and doctor's report, I was unable to claim for any government sickness benefit. I now had the necessary paperwork, and could at least receive some money to go towards living costs, although much of the medical and treatment costs were being met by my generous and willing parents. It was a psychological help to me to know that they weren't now supporting me completely.

That breakthrough visit to the doctor was only the beginning, however, of the long haul ahead. Despite the fact that my body now had the complete rest that it needed and was being treated for some of the symptoms, my health grew considerably worse over the following few months as it let down all its defences. Halting the flow of adrenaline that had kept me going until then and sensing that it no longer had to push on, my body crashed, well and truly.

I found it absolutely terrifying. Now struggling to walk to the bathroom and back, my morning shower sapped all the energy I had for the day. While I was bathing, Mum would put out fresh pyjamas and change the sheets on my bed, and then I would crawl back in, utterly wiped out. There was no indication of how much lower my body would sink or how long this illness would last.

From the Ends of the Earth

The only thing I really did know for sure was that it wasn't fatal. I have to say that I often didn't actually find this a comforting thought. I certainly didn't feel like I was living, and I couldn't look forward to dying (which, as a Christian, is not a fearful concept to me anyway); so it seemed that I was just suspended in this horrible state of merely 'existing', with hope for the future all but gone.

I longed for my weary body to fall asleep and not wake up. I certainly wasn't any good to anyone in the state I was in, I thought, not even to God, as I wasn't even around people for whom I could be an example or a help or to whom I could speak about Him. Clearly, as a driven perfectionist, my sense of purpose and value had been based more upon what I could achieve and do for God and for people than simply on who I was. Now that I could not *do* anything, I felt useless.

I struggled to see that I was no more or less valuable to God or to anyone else in my current state. The truth was my worth lay simply in the fact that God created me, but it would take me a long time to learn this lesson and not to feel that I was merely 'taking up space' or 'not paying my way in society'. For example, although I needed the money that my sickness benefit provided, it went totally against my grain to be receiving money that I hadn't earned.

Also entwined in this struggle were other issues, such as pride. I was used to being the capable one that others could turn to for help, as well as having the ability to accomplish many things in my own life without having to lean too much on others. I had developed a fiercely independent spirit that found it very hard to receive from others, even when they were longing for an opportunity to give. Adept at giving, I was now finding it very difficult to receive. God had to show me how selfish that was – unless I was willing to receive from others sometimes, I was denying them the blessing and the satisfaction of giving that I had enjoyed. I struggled with feelings of guilt that people had to now do things for me that I could not repay. Clearly I was being humbled in that area of my life.

Once a capable and driven high-achiever, I found it very difficult to feel 'out of control'. Although control over our lives is somewhat of an illusion – let's face it, who can possibly control every circumstance and every action of others? We're fooling ourselves if we think we can – I hadn't had to face too many situations in my life that really sent me into a tailspin. Yes, I had faced a number of childhood and teenage traumas that were very 'big' to me at the time, but nothing in my life had rocked my boat like this, and I was completely powerless to fix it.

I had no control over how my body would feel each day, if, and how, it would respond to medication, how long it would take to see any improvement, if this illness would last weeks, months, years or forever, if I would ever work again. Never had I been in a position where I couldn't do what I wanted simply by setting my mind to it and working hard, and it was very, very frightening. No amount of drive, motivation or self-discipline was of any use, and I didn't know how to cope.

I felt isolated from the rest of the world in a number of senses. For a start, I physically couldn't get out of my bed to do all the things I used to enjoy –sport, shopping, movies, church. It was as if I had suddenly dropped out of life. Contact with people became very limited, apart from my immediate family. Close friends were starting to scatter in pursuit of all the options available to young university graduates in their early twenties….making headway in careers, getting married, backpacking overseas, buying houses, having children. I know it wasn't necessarily that they didn't care about me, but we were young and they were busy and their lives were taking off, and I had an illness that few had heard of and even fewer understood.

At first I still received invitations to places and events, but as I had to keep refusing, the invitations understandably stopped coming. When I sank into self-pity, I was reminded that I had behaved the same way towards my friend from school who had been diagnosed with this illness several years earlier. I hadn't gone out of my way to visit, to send notes, to keep her in the loop with what was going on, and now I was experiencing what she must have gone through. Compassion certainly arises from shared suffering, and God was building in me through my own experiences empathy and understanding for the weak, the lonely and the sick.

Making the loneliness even more difficult to bear was the fact that although on the one hand I craved the company of my friends, on the other I was actually too ill to cope with visitors, at least in the early months. The effort of interaction with others (including my family) was more than I could make – in my fatigue, my brain often couldn't process information, put sentences together or cope with the noise of talk and laughter. As someone who had often been described by others as 'bubbly' and 'a people person', I found this incredibly distressing. This illness seemed not only to be robbing me of what I could do; it seemed to be stealing the essence of who I was.

Of course, I wasn't completely abandoned by everyone and a few precious friends stayed in touch, but Mum and Dad had to screen all my phone calls, and I could return some only when I had the energy for a short conversation. Much of the time I couldn't even cope with interacting with my parents and I spent my days, weeks, months in bed in my room with the door closed, shutting out the world.

Now is probably as good a time as any to pay tribute to my parents for all they gave and suffered at this time. Here was their twenty-two year old daughter, whom they had just put through five years of university, and who should have been established in a job and soon moving out of home. Instead, she had been able to last only four months in a job and was struck down with an illness that destroyed her ability to do anything much at all. Yet no one seemed to be able to give any answers. An adult daughter who should have been independent was now back under their roof, relying on them for basic needs and financial support.

Not once did they question the validity of my illness or suggest that it was all in my head; not once did they make me feel that I needed to hurry up and move out of their home; not once did they complain about the financial implications of my being there or of my medical treatment; not once was I made to feel that I was a burden or an interruption to their lives.

All this was taken for granted back then, because in my mind it was all about the awful experience that was happening to *me*, but years later at a party, I bumped into a girl I knew from uni. When she learned of my illness, her comment was that she didn't know what she would have done in that situation as her family circumstances meant that going back home to live wouldn't have been an option. I began to realise that my suffering was also my parents' suffering and that part of God's care for me was through the parents He gave me.

Mum changed and washed my bed linen and pyjamas almost every day, bought and cooked food that I fancied, and both Mum and Dad fielded all phone calls. Dad took the day off work to drive us to the doctor every fortnight, and he and Mum waited in the surgery with me (about two hours each time), then stopped to buy any medication I needed. They coped with my emotional instability – tears, outbursts of frustration, silences – and cried many tears with me and for me. All this and much, much more without a word of complaint or condemnation. Mostly, they prayed, and I know that those prayers had great effect, despite appearances, both then and in the years which have followed. I am sure that I would not have emerged from this trauma as strongly, or be doing what I am today without their prayers, and I am more thankful than words can express.

For most of the time it was just God and me and the four walls of my bedroom. Despite the utter fatigue and collapse of my body, and the overwhelming desire to sleep for six months straight, slumber would hardly come at all, a paradoxical symptom of ME. I dozed a bit but had little more than a few hours of broken sleep every twenty-four hours. That left a lot of time for thinking, when my brain could do it.

I went through a painful process of re-examining my faith. After a lifetime of love for and service to God, I struggled with feeling abandoned, let down, hurt and angry. My wonderful, loving, earthly parents would have done anything if it meant I would get well. I know that they felt powerless because they couldn't 'fix' a horrible situation for their child; yet my loving Heavenly Father seemed to be silent and inactive. He was the only one who could actually do something about it, so why didn't He?

One morning I woke up wondering what it would feel like to live as if there wasn't a God, or one who cared anyway. What if I had been living an illusion all these years in regard to my faith? I decided that I would see what it was like to pretend there was no God, and tried to push Him out of my mind. Maybe my suffering would be easier minus the spiritual struggle in which I was engaged.

Well, that was easily the biggest failure of an experiment that I have ever attempted! After more than fifteen years experiencing God's love, answers to prayer, and a dynamic relationship with Him, trying to pretend that He didn't exist just because He wasn't making Himself visible to me just then was like my trying to pretend that my Mum didn't exist because she wasn't in my bedroom right at that moment.

I had seen too much evidence of God in my own life to deny His existence. In fact, I couldn't even last ten minutes without pouring out hurt, anger and frustration to Him in my heart. I couldn't *not* communicate with Him, even if my communication was reduced to the raw emotions of anger or tears of grief. I *knew* He was still there and that He could still hear me. It might have felt like there was a ceiling between us, but His existence couldn't be denied.

My struggle switched focus from the issue of God's existence to the nature of His character. Who was God that He was not doing anything to answer my desperate pleas for help? Was He actually the caring, loving, compassionate and powerful God that I had spent my lifetime believing He was because that's who the Bible said He was? Or was He a remote and cold figure as some believed – either not taking action because He couldn't be bothered or because He didn't really like me very much?

Months went by as I lay in my bed and wrestled with these issues. They had to be resolved because there was no point continuing to live my life dedicated to Someone who was not the person I had believed Him to be.

My eyes had become so sensitive to light that my parents fitted venetian blinds to my bedroom windows to block out the harsh Queensland sunlight. Sore eyes and poor concentration on top of fatigue meant that I was unable to read anything much of the time, even my Bible, and so I purchased the Bible recorded on cassette. Sometimes out of hurt and disappointment with God I couldn't bear to think of reading or listening to His Word, but something in me still hungered for it and I couldn't abandon it entirely. So I played Bible tapes although I often dozed off as they played, and at times I wondered if it was much use to even play them when my brain couldn't follow them properly or I just fell asleep.

However, I don't believe any of that hearing of Scripture was wasted. God's Word is truth and power, and even if my conscious mind couldn't absorb or focus on it, my spirit and faith was being nourished. Many times in later years, God has brought Scriptures to my mind to speak to me in all sorts of situations; verses of the Bible that I have absolutely no recollection of consciously memorising. I know they come from those days on my sickbed when the Word of God was being implanted in my heart from those Bible cassettes. Although my faith seemed pretty weak and hanging by a thread back then, it was actually being fortified by listening to the Word of God.

One book that became particularly precious to me during this time was the old blue Presbyterian Church hymn book. Although about six years previously I had ceased regularly attending the church in which I grew up to attend one of a different denomination, the words of many of those well-known old hymns from my childhood struck a chord with my hurting heart. So many were birthed out of the deep grief and tragedy suffered by the authors.

One hymn in particular I could not read without weeping. It seemed as if everything about my current

Kathryn Kerridge

situation belied the words of the lyric, but I was drawn to it so often that I wrote down the words and put them in a photo frame. It hung at eye level on the wall against which my bed was positioned, and I would read it many times each day, knowing it was true, and holding on to the glimmer of hope that it gave me:

> *Be still my soul; the Lord is on your side*
> *Bear patiently the cross of grief or pain*
> *Leave to your God to order and provide*
> *Through every change He faithful will remain*
> *Be still my soul; thy best, thy heavenly friend*
> *Through thorny ways, leads to a joyful end.*
>
> *Be still my soul, your God will undertake*
> *To guide the future as He has the past.*
> *Your hope, your confidence, let nothing shake,*
> *All now mysterious shall be clear at last.*
> *Be still, my soul: the tempests still obey*
> *His voice, who ruled them once on Galilee.*
>
> *Be still, my soul: the hour is hastening on*
> *When we shall be forever with the Lord,*
> *When disappointment, grief and fear are gone,*
> *Sorrow forgotten, love's pure joy restored.*
> *Be still, my soul: when change and tears are past*
> *All safe and blessed we shall meet at last.*

(Katharina Von Schlegal 1752
Translated by Jane Borthwick 1855)

From the Ends of the Earth

To this day, I cannot hear that tune or sing that song in church without tears springing to my eyes. It is a reminder that God sees and is present in every pain of life, that He will continue to work through it, that this life is short and will pass – and what is most important is an eternal view that looks forward to the time when there will be *'no more death or sorrow or crying or pain' (Revelation 21:4 NLT)*. Until then, pain is a part of life and He is there to comfort us when it strikes.

A great encouragement at this time was my dog-eared copy of Joni Eareckson Tada's autobiography. At only seventeen, Joni broke her neck and became a quadriplegic after diving into shallow water. I had first read her story when I was at primary school, Mum had all her music tapes, and I remember hearing her speak at Brisbane's Festival Hall when I was about eight years old.

Joni's testimony was very well-known to me, but I had never identified with her story of physical suffering and spiritual searching more than I did at this time. My physical condition was nowhere near as serious as hers, of course, but our lives as we knew them had come to a devastating end, and she too, spent many, many hours on her own in her bed searching out answers to her questions about who God was, what His purposes were, and His will and actions regarding physical healing. Her documented struggles and her pain were written with a raw honesty that was of great comfort to me.

Kathryn Kerridge

God brought another source of encouragement to my bedside. A friend of the family had heard that there was a 'Christian video man' who drove a van around with Christian videos for hire. Mum and Dad had bought a little television for my room and put the family video recorder there as well to help me while away my sleepless days and nights. The video man, Brian, became a weekly visitor and good friend. Once a week, in my pyjamas and dressing gown I went down to the van to make my selections. I was encouraged by a number of movies, video recordings of Christian artists' concerts, and even children's animated features, all with Biblical content. Some spoke so directly to my circumstances that I borrowed them time after time till I knew parts off by heart. And so God sustained me with His Word in a form which I was able to accept and absorb.

Brian sometimes joined us for lunch or coffee at our kitchen table. With one of those 'darkness to light' adult conversion experiences, tattoos and scars told the story of some of his previous life experiences. Brian's faith was real and honest, and he didn't spout the Christian clichés that were frequently offered simply because people didn't know what to say. Like the visits from my Blue Nurses, Brian's company was comforting and healing.

God was touching my life with people who had been through suffering themselves and didn't have all the answers; people who didn't judge or trundle out advice; just ordinary people who loved me, accepted me, listened to me and shared in my struggles. He brought into my life people who could understand and cope with what I was going through, and who would show me His love and care when I didn't sense it coming from God Himself.

Despite my hurting soul and struggling faith, I knew deep down that God had a good grip on me in this dark time. He was patiently receiving all my questions, all my angry and frustrated outbursts, all my tears, and all my unjust accusations against Him. I was like a tiny child beating little fists in frustration and rage against the huge chest of a strong father; and God was just like that loving Father, taking all that my puny strength could give out, waiting until I finally fell exhausted into His arms so He could just hold me and love me and help me understand what He was doing.

God was asking for my trust – for me to trust that He knew and cared about what was happening to me; to trust that He had the power to heal and was not impotent in any situation; to trust that He could truly make all things in my life, even the most awful ones, work for my good in His time and in His way; and to trust that He was seeing a picture far greater than I could ever see or understand.

The bottom line for me became as simple as this: I could doubt God, decide He wasn't worth following, forsake my faith and subsequently live my life according to my own terms, making decisions according to my own understanding and desires. However, making that decision wasn't going to make my illness disappear, and it seemed to me far more hopeless and desperate to live my life with this sickness and prognosis *without* God than it would be to endure it knowing that God was not only with me for comfort and guidance but could and would work it into something positive in my life.

Like that exhausted child who finally grows weary of fighting, at some point during these months I stopped 'beating my puny fists against God's chest'. There was a lot I didn't know about what was going on or why, or what was going to happen to me, or what kind of future I had, but I *did* know certain things. I did know that God existed; I did know that He wasn't indifferent, vindictive or powerless; and I did know that nothing could happen to me that He couldn't turn around for His good purposes in my life. Therefore, my future was not hopeless, my life was not useless, and my suffering was not pointless.

God was teaching me that living a life of faith requires living with mysteries, and those truths about God that I did know would be enough to carry me through any circumstance in life that was full of the unknown. If my God could create the universe with only words from His mouth; if He could calm storms and heal sickness and raise the dead, as Jesus demonstrated; if He could do all that the Bible reveals that He can, then not only is He not obliged to answer to me as to what He allows into my life and why, but I wouldn't be able to understand all His higher purposes if He were to try to explain them to me anyway.

Like Job of the Bible, I had come to the point where I could say that no matter what happens…*'yet will I trust Him' (Job 13:15; NKJV*, emphasis mine). I identified so much with this man's story of suffering as he, too, wrestled with his understanding of God and His purposes. Time after time was this book of the Bible my companion during my year of confinement – Job's words of pain and lament verbalised what I was feeling in my heart and crying in my tears but couldn't put into words myself. The very inclusion of that book in God's Word was proof to me that God knew and understood the pain of human suffering, the questions it raises about Him and the universe, and how He desires to put that into perspective with who He is and what His purposes are, demolishing many of our human arguments and accusations along the way.

Part of my spiritual journey at this time included repentance of my own attitudes and mindsets, sometimes towards other people, but particularly towards God Himself. Yes, it was absolutely true that my pain and illness was awful, was not my fault, and was out of my control, but what was within my control was whether I chose to believe and act out of faith in the truth of God's Word or not. The 'not' times were, quite baldly, sin, and I had to apologise to God for those times if I was to continue to have a clear and unbroken relationship with Him.

I stopped crying out to God so much for answers to my 'why' and 'what' and 'when' questions (although they were still very much there and surfaced from time to time), and my prayer became a much quieter heartfelt plea that this devastation of my life would not be wasted, that God would use it in some way to help others or to point others to Him. I wouldn't say that I had yet reached James' stage of counting it 'pure joy' (James 1:2, NIV) that I was experiencing this trial, but at least I was now seeing it less as all about *me* and *my* comfort and what *I* wanted for my life, and more as a vehicle that God could use for *His* purposes and *His* glory, and to enable me to reach out more to others in their need.

I remember as a child and teenager hearing the testimonies at churches or youth events of people who had experienced radical conversions – from alcoholism, or drug addiction, or atheism to Christianity – and how God had dramatically turned their lives and behaviour around in a short time. I used to think, 'Wow – I wish I had a testimony!' Clearly I didn't have the correct understanding that a Christian 'testimony' is simply a personal story of what God has done in a life, whether quick and dramatic, or slowly and steadily as had been the case in my own life.

From the Ends of the Earth

One day as I was lying in my bed having one of my conversations with God about why He was allowing all this to happen to me, an answer came to my mind immediately, 'Well, you always wanted a testimony, and now I'm giving you one!' It was as clear as if God was standing next to me saying it in an audible voice (which He wasn't) and I could almost hear Him saying this with a smile on His face...Be careful what you wish for, you might just get it!

My trust in God still felt pretty raw and tentative at this point; my faith had been utterly shaken as my life was turned upside down, but that was no bad thing. My faith, although an integral part of my life for seventeen years, still needed testing to develop maturity, strength, patience and endurance, and mine had never been through such an intense refining fire until this point.

There was a lot more work to be done to build up my relationship with God again, and for my trust to be as absolute as it needed to be. However, I knew that having my heart and faith stripped bare in that dark bedroom in my lonely hours had forced me to really 'count the cost' of following God in a way that I couldn't possibly have done when I first decided to be a Christian at the age of five. There was nothing 'wrong' with my childhood faith - in fact, it was that solid foundation and a lifetime of knowledge and experience of God that I was falling back on now – it's just that God was taking my faith a whole lot deeper by way of this period of suffering, but boy, did it hurt!

I really did want more than anything to follow God's will for my life and to know Him more by whatever means God chose to allow that to happen. I wanted to become more Christ-like in character, to enable Him to show Himself more clearly through me; it's just that this method wasn't what I had in mind, and quite frankly I wasn't enjoying the process. Although learning to be more submissive to His purposes, there were times I did it kicking and screaming, while God, like the patient Father He is, simply waited for me to stop my tantrum so He could do something useful with me. I learnt that in life's tests, the only way out is through, and as I focused my energy on the journey through, I experienced the calmness and peace to see and understand more clearly what God was doing in me, with me and for me, and even a little bit of the 'why'.

Although I still felt quite distant from God at this point – I guess I was holding Him a bit warily at arm's length, if one can do that with God – I somehow knew that my faith *was* stronger although it didn't feel like it yet, and as a result of these months of soul and faith searching, I would never again need to question His existence or His love for me. That's not to say I would no longer ask questions about faith issues or what and why things were going on in my life, but I would do so *with* a heart that was much more secure in the knowledge of who God is.

The rebuilding process of my side of our relationship would take a few years yet, but it had started on a foundation that had been stripped bare, that had been tested and would stand firm.

Issues of healing were the subject of much of my soul-searching, wondering, reading and praying at this time. Did I believe that God could heal me? Absolutely! Did I pray for my healing? Yes, a lot! I wanted nothing more than to be well again. I prayed; my family and friends prayed; I was anointed with oil and prayed for; and I believed in faith. And yet day after day, I remained confined to bed, suffering through this illness. I searched my heart for hidden sin, I wondered if my faith wasn't strong enough.

In the end, I had to leave it with God and realise that I could not demand anything from Him. He wanted me to pray; He wanted me to have faith; but only He knew His higher purposes and I had to leave the answers and results to Him and trust. The bottom line is that He is God and I am not! I will never understand Him, but that's what makes Him worth entrusting my life to. Would I really want to follow a God whom I could completely comprehend and who would simply accede to my demands as I saw life from my own small point of view?

God had said He was giving me a testimony, and it wasn't going to be too much longer before I saw the beginning of what He had in mind. Even as I questioned Him and wrestled with Him in my spiritual life, He was beginning to guide me on a path that would seem too bizarre to be possible. Out of what appeared to be the wreckage of my life, He was soon to resurrect a long-held, but buried, dream, and then later follow it with international ministry opportunities that would span the globe. However, I wouldn't see this come to fruition until many years later. For now, God was going to ask me to take a step of faith to get me into the practice of obeying His calling to do seemingly crazy and impossible things...

Chapter 5

The end of 1993 was drawing close. What a nightmare of a year! Despite my diagnosis and treatments and although my health seemed to be 'bottoming out' after a period of further decline, still I was able to do very little at all. My morning routine had been reduced to a shower, changing into fresh pyjamas, and crawling back into bed. That little exercise often used up all my day's energy supply. After months of inactivity, the muscles that had been so worked by years of regular sport up had lost their tone and strength, and months of lying horizontal in bed had reduced the efficiency of my heart in pumping blood around my body, worsening the feelings of physical weakness.

I was desperate for some sort of hope for the future, to know that this was not a picture of the rest of my life. From a medical point of view, there was no cure for ME, and no clear prognosis. Some people seemed to eventually get back to living a degree of normal life, some stayed at a reduced level of life for years and years, some were never able to work or function normally again. I pleaded with God for a glimmer of light in this dark tunnel. Wasn't there *something* I could aim for, something I could look forward to – anything but this?

Kathryn Kerridge

One day, I received an answer to my pleadings. It came quite clearly to my mind – "Camp Counselors USA". It was the name of an American summer camp recruitment organisation. God was about to resurrect a 'dead' dream of mine in the most extraordinary way.

I have written that I never felt that I had a particular calling to be a missionary. However, for a very long time, I'd had a strong fascination for the USA. Because my mental image of 'mission' work involved non-English speaking, often third world countries, I never really thought of my penchant for the America as a missionary calling.

As far back as primary school, I had a deep interest in the United States; at eleven I had an American pen pal, and I loved hearing and reading about the country – history, geography, travel, and lifestyle. I relished any American history, geography and literature we studied at high school, and devoured the articles and photos that appeared every month in the 'National Geographic' magazine. A number of American exchange students came to our high school, and in my senior year our SU group was visited by an American Teen Mission team. I was incredibly drawn towards talking to them and even stayed in touch with some for a while afterwards.

At university, my Arts degree included several American history subjects and it was an absolute pleasure researching for assignments and studying

From the Ends of the Earth

for exams (well, maybe not always a 'pleasure', but I didn't find it as tedious as some other subjects).

Several Christian friends were discovering callings to pursue mission work in places like Africa, India, and Thailand, and I considered my interest in the States just that – a personal interest. After all, America was a land of plenty and opportunity, with churches and Christian organisations galore. Why would they need missionaries from overseas?

In my first year at uni, I saw a poster in the student union building advertising jobs at American summer camps, and I remember immediately thinking '*That's* what I want to do one day!' I was passionate about week-long SU holiday camps in Queensland – what bliss to be at camp for three months straight and in the USA to boot!

The difficulty was, of course, in living in the southern hemisphere where summer was December through to February, and not June through August. In order to spend three months at an American summer camp, I would have to take an entire year off university, as the northern summer cut through both semesters of the Australian university academic year. I was sure that God had directed me towards the next five years of university for my Arts/Law degree, and as my parents were very much helping me financially through this, taking a whole year off to indulge a dream wasn't an option.

Still, I filed away the idea in my mind, thinking that if it was still there at the end of my degree, maybe I could pursue it after graduation prior to getting a job and 'settling down'.

By my final year of university, however, jobs in law firms were getting more difficult to obtain. By that point there were about twice as many law students graduating each year as there were articled clerk positions on offer in Queensland. Even allowing for graduates who would take their careers in other directions, this meant that employment became a higher priority than taking a few months off to go to an American summer camp. Perhaps this was one of those personal dreams that wasn't in God's plan for me after all. I accepted that and assumed the desire would fade away. Strangely though, the desire, instead of lessening, remained strong.

But here I was years later, bedridden and exhausted, asking God for hope to go on, and this thought comes like an arrow to my mind, completely out of the blue. Admittedly, my first reaction was, 'Not fair, God! You know that dream meant so much to me.' To taunt me with it now when I was so ill and obviously unable to contemplate such a thing seemed almost cruel. I rejected the thought. God wasn't callous so maybe it was the devil or my own mind taunting me with a carrot that was out of reach.

However, after weeks of the idea insistently returning to my mind, I started to wonder if this idea really *was* from God. In my years of living as a Christian and learning to hear His voice and follow His leading, I knew enough about the process to know that it was not in my interests to ignore Him. It wouldn't hurt to phone for an application form and some more information, ridiculous as it seemed. When the paperwork arrived in the mail, I began to fill out the form, bit by bit each day.

One evening during this process, I dressed to go with Mum and Dad to a CCUSA information meeting in the city. My parents had been informed as to what I had been thinking, and I still remember the look that crossed Mum's face as I spoke – only she knows exactly what she was thinking at the time, but her face seemed to me to express a combination of panic and of wondering if I had completely lost my mind in the trauma of my illness.

I am so thankful for my parents' response. They said very little at my announcement but prayed fervently, and supported me from the very beginning. If this indeed was God prompting me, then no matter how absurd it seemed, they were not going to stand in my way or discourage me (although I'm sure Mum felt like chaining me to my bed until I was completely better to stop me doing anything foolish with this stubborn, driven nature of mine).

The first thing the camp representative stressed at the meeting was that contrary to popular belief, a summer at camp was not a cheap and easy way to

Kathryn Kerridge

travel around the USA. If we heard or saw anything (on the films they showed) that made us doubt we would enjoy or be prepared to undertake the work involved in being a camp counsellor, then we were probably not right for the job. At that, I was starting to feel a little worried that my idea was indeed a crackpot one after all.

Immediately the first film began and I saw the images of American kids and teenagers playing, laughing, eating, singing, and working together at camp, I was so filled with emotion that I would have left right there and then if there was a plane waiting outside the door! My heart swelled with an overwhelming desire to be there, especially when I saw one of the camp 'toys' that was shown. It was called a 'Blob' and was a huge air-filled pillow which floated on a lake. One person sat on the end facing open water, and another person jumped from a tower onto the other end, launching the first person in the air to splashdown into the water. It looked amazing, but the representative said that only a few camps on their books had a Blob, therefore it was not sufficient motivation and we shouldn't hold out high hopes of being at a camp with one!

Every single thing I heard and saw that evening was throwing another log on the fire already burning in my heart, and I whispered to Mum and Dad that I just *knew* that I was meant to do this. The whole evening was like a confirmation from God that I was on the right track, even though the effort of that excursion wiped me out physically for days afterwards.

So I was on the right track to a direction for the future, but what about the timing? It seemed absurd to think that this was part of the plan for the following year; could it be for later on perhaps? That was a sensible possibility, but even as I was filling out the application form, I felt more strongly that I was meant to apply for the following year.

Part of the application form included questions relating to health, and I honestly answered that I had been diagnosed with this medical condition, was undergoing treatment, and expected that I would be in a position to go to camp in another eight months. Did I really believe that, I wondered? Oh well, the outcome of this was up to God anyway. If the organisation didn't like my application, the answer would be no, and if God wanted me there, He would arrange it. I didn't dare tell my doctor I was planning this – she would have been furious and I could imagine that telling her that I felt God was asking me to do this would go down like a lead balloon! It still sounded bizarre even to me.

After an interview, I was accepted into the CCUSA programme, and awaited a placement. Although I could express my camp preference on the application form (private camp, Jewish camp, church camp, day camp, Girl Guide camp etc), once my application was accepted I had no further say and was obliged to accept the offer I was made. I simply couldn't imagine camp with children where I wouldn't be free to tell them about Jesus, so my fervent prayer was that all my listed church and SU experience would cause me to be put in the 'church camp' category. To me, this was a mission trip – my whole motivation was for it to be an extension of what I felt my ministry calling was – to communicate information about God's love to children in the context of a camp, as I had been so passionately doing with SU Queensland. This time I would get three months of it in one hit, which I wasn't able to do at home.

Just before Christmas, notification came in the mail of my placement at a Presbyterian summer camp near Lancaster, Ohio, called 'Geneva Hills'. When I looked up our World Book Encyclopaedia to read up more about Ohio, I discovered that the State motto is 'With God, All Things are Possible'. You can't tell me that God doesn't have a sense of humour!

Up on the wall opposite my bed went a huge National Geographic map of the United States of America. After facing this map every day, I could have easily filled in a blank map of the USA with all the state boundaries and capital cities! On my good days, I really could believe that God would have me well enough in time to go; on my bad days, I couldn't believe that I'd even had the audacity to send the application in – what was I thinking?! All I could do was be patient and wait.

The months continued and gradually I was able to see some forward progress in my health. Into the New Year, after my daily morning shower I dressed properly instead of getting back into my pyjamas, and this went a long way to making me feel a bit more 'normal'. I was able to sit up for short periods, to write letters, or do some craft work, and was more able to cope with people. I spent more time on the phone, although I still wasn't able to leave the house much.

Due to illness disrupting my articled clerkship and professional subjects, I needed another ten credit points to officially graduate with my law degree. I chose 'Comparative Law' a subject which interested me and which involved attendance of only one lecture a week at uni. Reading the materials and writing my papers for a few hours a week could be done from home and gave me something concrete to focus on. Besides, the course content considered other countries' legal systems. With a large freedom of choice for our two assignment topics, I chose as one a discussion of a constitutional issue in the American legal system.

By Easter 1994, I dared to try my health at a week-long (Monday to Friday) SU primary camp. This would be a real test – the most taxing thing my body had attempted for twelve months.

It felt so incredibly good to be using my gifts and fulfilling my passion for working with children, and I was very blessed with the new friends I made among the other team members. This camp provided my first real opportunity to testify about my illness and how God was helping me cope with it.

Each day during the Bible teaching programme, a leader was asked to speak for a few minutes on how they became a Christian and what God has done for them. When my turn came, I stood in front of the campers with a row of lighted candles on a nearby table.

I explained that I had decided to follow Jesus at a very young age, and always felt very close to Him through my prayers and the ways He had blessed and helped me. Then I became sick, so sick that I couldn't get out of bed very much for almost a whole year (their little eyes widened!). I wasn't able to do any of the things that I had loved and had been like lights in my life – I had to give up my job, going out with my friends, going to church and youth group, playing sport, going to SU camps.

As I listed each one of these, I blew out one of the candles until they were all extinguished. I explained to the children that it seemed like all the lights in my life had gone out and everything was really dark and scary, but that there was one light in my life that remained. I brought out a big picture of the sun. Just as no person could ever blow out the light of the sun as they could a candle, God was the one source of light in my life that was constant and wouldn't ever run low, and no matter how awful things in my life had become, God was always there to love me and look after me and help me through. Although there are times when it seems that the sun is unseen, hidden behind a thick lot of grey storm clouds, that didn't mean it wasn't there the whole time.

As I was speaking, I experienced such a sense of thankfulness for this opportunity to share the reality of God's faithfulness and love. Sure, I still could have spoken about my faith had my life continued to run fairly smoothly, but there was something more meaningful about testifying to these things after a time of trial.

The week at camp did tax my health substantially, but I had made it through although it took me a while to recover. I tried not to think too much about the fact that a summer at an American camp would mean about ten of these weeks back to back. How on earth would I manage that?

One thing I had to do was buy a backpack for my trip. I went to a local camping store, where a helpful saleswoman eyed me up and produced a pack suitable for my height and size. Oh my, but it looked *far* too small to take everything that I would need for four whole months! I asked to see the biggest backpack they had. The woman looked at me doubtfully but brought out a twenty-five litre red and grey one. Even this one didn't look all that big to me, but it felt alright on my back. (Yeah, right – it extended from the tip of my head way down to just past my bottom!) How funny it seems now that I thought I could carry this very far fully loaded…I didn't know much about 'travelling light'.

Right! I had my backpack, visa and stash of Vegemite. Just a couple more months in which to gain some more strength and I would be ready to go.

And so it was that on June 3, 1994, I was at the airport with my family and a number of faithful friends, ready to board my QANTAS flight to Los Angeles. Looking back, I wonder at the faith and risk involved in the course of action I was about to take, and I have no explanation except to say that it must have been God who showed me what He wanted me to do and then gave me the faith and capacity to follow through on His leading, because it still seems like a pretty crazy thing to undertake.

My assumption was that at some point in this adventure God was going to completely heal my body of ME. After all, from my point of view, there was no other way I was going to survive the next four months without collapsing unless He did. I had never experienced a whole summer of camps before, but I knew what a one-week SU camp did to one's energy – to multiply that by twelve with minimal time to rest in between was simply inconceivable without good health.

From the Ends of the Earth

Physically I felt no different waiting at the airport to board the plane – excited, yes, but still with that ever-present ME fatigue. Maybe the healing would come as I walked onto the plane….maybe I'd be restored completely as I slept during the flight….maybe as I walked off the plane in Los Angeles. It was up to God, really, but of course it would happen within the next day or two. It had to, or I reckoned they'd be sending me back home on a stretcher!

I arrived in LA to find that none of my hopes had materialised. I felt just the same, only much wearier after a long and sleepless plane journey added to jet-lag.

After a twenty-four hour orientation period with other Australian camp counsellors at the Loyola Marymount University campus in LA, I spent a further couple of days on my own exploring Santa Monica before flying to Columbus, Ohio. I was off to the Midwestern USA, the farthest away I had ever lived from the ocean.

At Columbus airport I was welcomed by the camp director, John, with a gigantic bear hug. After my luggage was stowed in the trunk of the car, I immediately embarrassed myself by waiting on the driver's side for the door to be unlocked, completely forgetting that Americans drive on the opposite side of the road! John asked with a grin if I wanted to drive, but I hastily scampered around to the passenger side, red-faced. During the journey to the camp centre, I discovered that in his twenties John had spent two years travelling Australia and New Zealand with a drama group, so we had some immediate common ground, apart from our Christian faith.

That was the first of many small details that God had taken into account in placing me at Geneva Hills – so many things about the site and how the programme was run perfectly suited my interests and desires; but why should I be surprised at that? When God is in something, there is nothing He leaves undone. John's whole family embraced me with an incredibly warm welcome - from hugs of greeting upon entering their home, to a later invitation to share in a family holiday after the summer was over. I was delighted to be there, finally living the dream I had cherished in my heart for so long, but there was some gnawing trepidation too.

I'd been in the USA four days and was certain I was exactly where God had led me to be, but my body was so indescribably weary. Even a healthy person would be tired as a result of jetlag, lack of sleep, and a busy four days, but add ME to the mix and I felt really done in. I hadn't even *started* what I'd actually gone there to do.

All of a sudden, the summer ahead looked very long and arduous, and quite a scary prospect. Australia and the comfort and support of home were thousands of miles away - how on earth would I physi-

From the Ends of the Earth

cally endure the next four months of responsibilities and demands of being a camp counsellor? Still, I had sought God every step of the way, and He had had plenty of opportunities to block my coming here if it wasn't in His will. I had to trust in the character of God – He doesn't set us up to fail – and just take one day at a time.

Two weeks of training ensued, during which I met and bonded with my fellow counsellors, a dozen friendly young Americans. Some had just completed high school and some were college students, and all welcomed me warmly. One girl with whom I shared a room in the staff quarters was quite concerned about the fact that my backpack of clothes and shoes was 'all' I had with me for four whole months, so she brought me a bag of clothes from home to supplement my wardrobe.

After training, the summer season began in earnest. Campers arrived on a Sunday afternoon and departed the following Saturday morning. We had a different age group each week, and I was tickled to see that camper accommodation was in covered wagons with bunk beds inside! God's sense of humour again, considering all my American history assignments, one of which was about the pioneering of the American West. Now I would be sleeping in a covered wagon each night – sure, they didn't go anywhere as there were no wheels, just stumps to anchor them to the ground, but they had canvas canopies overhead, and there was a campfire ring in

Kathryn Kerridge

the middle of each group of four wagons over which to toast marshmallows and make 's'mores'. (To make a 's'more', take a toasted marshmallow and a square of chocolate and sandwich them between sweet crackers. Then eat and enjoy the whole sticky mess! Mmmm...!)

Every evening, the whole camp joined together to sing praise songs around the campfire. I loved to sing and this was easily my favourite time of day – the atmosphere of worship around the fire under the night sky was amazing. In fact we sang a lot; after most meals as well as at campfire, and I never tired of it. Another sign to me that God had been behind every detail of my placement.

The site itself was 360 acres of beauty and fun – incorporating a small lake with canoes and paddle-boats (but no Blob!), a pool, a log cabin for arts and crafts, a high ropes course, a climbing wall, a couple of dining rooms, various forms of accommodation, and miles of hiking trails through the woods.

The aim of Geneva Hills was to create a positive camp experience that would point the campers towards God and for those that already had a Christian faith, to help them to grow and mature in that faith. It fitted perfectly with my own personal mission for camping and my experience of working with Scripture Union in Queensland. Even the number of campers was similar – a weekly average of around forty to fifty, rather than several hundred,

From the Ends of the Earth

as some big summer camps had. I really couldn't have imagined a better placement. Every day as I hiked, swam, did crafts, sang, played, and spoke with my young people about Jesus as well as the ordinary stuff of life, I was constantly reminded of the amazing power of God to resurrect dreams from the dead and to make the impossible possible.

Puzzling to me, though, was that I was as tired as ever and all of my ME symptoms were very much present. I had certainly expected God to heal my body so that I could get through the summer and then resume my life back home, but every morning when I arose, my body was a bit more weary than the day before and I often plodded along on what seemed like nothing more than a combination of adrenalin and sheer force of will. I was eating healthily and John delivered my weekly vitamin injection into my arm, but I was definitely *not* sailing through as I had expected. I was dependent upon God just for the energy to work every day, and although I wasn't overflowing with it, He was true to His promise of supplying my need. Weeks had passed and I had not collapsed, caught any other illnesses, or been unable to fulfil my duties. However, I wished that I was not so exhausted so that I could enjoy my days more. Some days I was so desperately tired that my whole body was in pain struggling to keep pace with the campers; I had to cry out to God for extra patience so I wouldn't snap at them because I was at the end of my rope.

Mum and Dad phoned every Sunday afternoon before the next camp group arrived, and more than once I remember saying to them that I didn't know what I was doing there, I was so exhausted, and did I really hear God directing me to come? They continued to pray and pray and pray – goodness knows how they felt after those phone conversations, especially after nursing me the previous year – but they continued to support and encourage me and pray. Doubtless their faithful and consistent prayers supplied much of the fuel that kept me going.

So no instant and miraculous healing then. It wasn't until a long time after the summer was over and I was back in Australia that I understood the nature of the miracle that God had worked in my life and body. It would have been far easier and more comfortable for the ME to have disappeared overnight, but God had different plans. He was more interested in stretching my faith and showing through the weakness of my body the greatness of His power and love. How much more of a miracle it was for God to take a weak and exhausted body that had been completely bedridden the year before, and sustain me through an intense and relentless (albeit very enjoyable) three months of camps. Every moment of every day, I had no choice but to ask for His strength and rely on His energy for every footstep.

Yes, I was weary and I struggled many days; yes, I had to spend many days off in my bed instead of with the other staff; yes, I was in pain and discomfort. Nevertheless I was living a dream I had long treasured in my heart, fulfilling a ministry and obeying my God. And yes, God blessed me every day – with the beauty of the site; with enough energy to swim, play and walk as much as the campers needed me to; with the constant encouragement of His presence; and with the love, compassion, generosity and friendship of the other staff. The expected healing did not come, but neither did God let me down. He is the God of the unexpected – both in terms of what He doesn't do, but also in terms of what He does do, and while I admit to being disappointed that He hadn't removed this disease, I was definitely *not* going to be disappointed as to what He was going to do next!

I had come to America with a list of things I would love to see and do after camp was over, including the famous landmarks of the USA – Grand Canyon, Niagara Falls, New York City, Disneyland. With four weeks of visa remaining after my camp commitments, the plan was to do some solo backpacking, hopping on and off buses and trains. I had spent months avidly reading my travel guide to the USA and didn't think this would be too difficult.

However, apart from being too exhausted after camp to cope with solo travel, I had underestimated the logistical difficulties. The USA is a huge country, public transport is not always readily available, and bus and train stations were sometimes in unsavoury parts of town. Money was also an issue – the 'pocket money' I earned over the summer only covered half my airfare costs, and all extra travel expenses and spending money was coming from my savings. I soon realised that travelling across the country on my own was not a viable option.

Strangely enough, I wasn't terribly disappointed at this realisation. I had come to America to follow God's call to a summer camp and to share and show His love to American children and teenagers as I had always wanted to do, and that was exactly what had occurred – mission accomplished! By all natural reasoning I shouldn't have lasted a week, yet I was still standing, and if I never saw anything of the USA other than Ohio and a little bit of California and Michigan as I had done, that was absolutely fine. I was welcome to stay with John's family for my remaining time in the States, inhabiting their basement room with another staff girl, and I was all set to rest and recover and be a part of this loving and warm household for a while longer, enjoying the beautiful site at my leisure.

However, God had other, far more wonderful plans in store, proving the Biblical principal that when we seek first His kingdom and make obedience to Him our primary concern, He adds so many more unexpected blessings to our lives.

John and his wife, Fay, were motorcycle enthusiasts and had organised a motorbike road trip to conclude the summer season. This year, the plan was a three-day ride to Niagara Falls and back. As end of summer neared, their children (Zach, Rachel and Joel) talked frequently about the upcoming trip, excited that ten year old Zach was joining the adult riders this year (as a pillion passenger of course). Considering that it would be great fun for me to go too, and undaunted by the fact that I didn't own a motorbike, eight year old Rachel suggested that I should just ask her dad about going along. In the end, I can't remember who asked, but the result was that I joined the group, riding on the back of a Honda Goldwing. It felt rather like enjoying panoramic views from the comfort of an armchair. My biggest fear was that I would be lulled to sleep and tumble off.

Our route passed through the north-eastern corner of West Virginia, Pennsylvania, and then into New York State, where we stopped over for the night. Unused to motorbikes, I at first hung on with a vice-like grip, but soon relaxed into the ride, leaning into the corners and enjoying the gorgeous scenery.

The following day, we crossed the Peace Bridge into Canada, pausing for another stamp in my passport. Back on the US side of Niagara Falls we boarded the 'Maid of the Mist' boat, donned blue plastic raincoats, and chugged to the base of the Falls. The sheer size and noise were absolutely astounding – no words can convey the magnitude of the sight and sound. Here I was at one of the tourist spots on my list – and I travelled here on the back of a motorbike in the company of a wonderful new group of Christian friends. Only God could possibly have arranged something like that. Little did I know there was much more to come hot on the heels of this little adventure.

The children had been talking all summer about their upcoming family holiday to the Grand Canyon. A two-week vacation had been planned around the date of a cousin's wedding in Colorado, departing the day after the motorcycle trip had ended.

At a rest stop on the ride home from Niagara, John and Fay approached me with the idea that since they were going to be doing such a great road trip across the country would I like to join them? I was stunned at this generous offer. I knew that the demands of a camping ministry made family vacation time especially precious; to share it with me was no small thing. Furthermore, the family car was too small to transport me as well as their three children, so a larger vehicle would have to be borrowed. I knew the offer was genuine and heartfelt, and I accepted with deep thanks. My travel itinerary was certainly being engineered by God.

A day and a backpack re-pack later I was settled into the back of a borrowed van along with Zach, Rachel and six year old Joel. Driving west, our route took us through Ohio, Indiana, Illinois, Missouri, Kansas and into Colorado for the family wedding. Never mind

From the Ends of the Earth

the fact that I was a complete stranger to these people, I was welcomed into the home and to the wedding as if I was a long lost friend.

The holiday was filled with amazing experiences against the backdrop of a stunning array of scenery and locations – hikes in the majestic Colorado mountains; the adobe architecture of Santa Fe, New Mexico; a native American pueblo in Taos, New Mexico; ancient ruins of a native American civilisation in Mesa Verde, Colorado; the Arizona desert; Monument Valley, Utah; a few relaxing days with family friends at a mountain ranch near Aspen, Colorado; and the highlight of it all, the magnificent Grand Canyon.

Arriving at Grand Canyon National Park one evening we were just in time to watch the sun set over this magnificent mile-high, mile-wide 'hole' in the earth. The Colorado River seemed a mere winding thread at the bottom. What an incredible 'wow!' moment that simply defies description and the effort of a camera to capture its size and beauty.

The plan was to get a good night's sleep and then hike the canyon the next day. Amply supplied with a picnic lunch, lots of chocolate for energy (boy, was I going to need it!) and as much water as we could carry, we set off at about 7.00am. Only then did we notice signs recommending hikers do *not* attempt the return trip in one day, but instead arrange to stay overnight at the campground or the hotel at the bottom. Too late – we had made no such bookings. Besides, I was in the company of the ultimate wilderness adventuring family to whom outdoor pursuits were a way of life. I was rather more concerned with my ability to keep up with *them*. Oh well, God had kept my ME-weakened body going through a summer of camp, what was a hike to the bottom of the world's largest canyon and back?! Besides, it didn't look all that bad from the top, really, and before I became ill, I was healthy, fit and active. All those miles of walking with Mum and playing volleyball had to count for something, surely!

The South Kaibab trail into the Canyon was six miles long. Searing heat filled the air and created a sensation of unrelenting thirst as the sun moved high in the sky, but thankfully, much of the trail followed the shade of the rock. Water supplies had to be eked out between tap points, and the regular sips seemed to take the edge off our thirst for only a few seconds. Groups of tourists riding donkeys passed us by. Walking would take longer and use more of our energy, but I didn't even think to envy the riders as I watched the donkeys' jolting backs. No doubt my legs would be stiff as a board the next day, but I was sure that my backside wouldn't be nearly as sore as the donkey riders' bottoms!

Lunch in the shade by Bright Angel Creek, followed by a dip, fully-clothed, in the cool refreshing water rejuvenated our bodies and our spirits. I felt pretty

From the Ends of the Earth

exhausted, but was on a high – had I *really* just hiked to the bottom of the Grand Canyon?

Bright Angel Trail back up to the rim was about nine miles long, a series of seemingly endless switchbacks. I don't think I'd gone half a mile before the novelty of being in the depths of one of the natural wonders of the world had completely worn off. What was I thinking? This was basically a nine-mile walk through the desert…*uphill*! Sometimes I could have sat down and cried from sheer exhaustion (the uncomfortable donkey rides looked like armchair luxury to me now), but I could hardly quit on everyone else and ask them to carry me. That request from the children was already being regularly fobbed off by their mum and dad.

Head down. Trudge on. One step, another step. Very thirsty. Sip of water. Stiff and sore, I urged my feet on through the red dust of the trail in the midday sun, numb to anything but the heat and my insatiable thirst. Would the top ever come? Goodness knows how Moses managed to lead more than a million Israelites through the wilderness for forty years!

Eight interminable hours later, in the cool of the evening, we reached the rim of the Canyon. Utterly spent, the magnitude of my achievement completely failed to register – just then, the Canyon looked a bit like an unfriendly monster that had sucked the life out of me. To be honest, I really didn't care about how immense and amazing it was.

Kathryn Kerridge

For much of the trek, I had been focused only on putting one foot in front of the other to keep up with the family. Occasionally, one of the children would whine a bit or beg to be carried, but they did a stellar job in keeping up, considering their ages. I gritted my teeth and thought to myself that if these children could do it, then I had to be able to. John and Fay appeared to be trekking along with ease due to their high fitness levels. Years later, when we reminisced about this trip, I discovered that as I had been spurred on by the example of children aged six, eight and ten, their mother had been gritting her teeth and thinking that if *I* was doing this with ME, then *she* had to be able to. We had to laugh.

The next morning, we slowly and painfully rolled ourselves stiffly out of bed and caught the Canyon shuttle bus around the west rim. The awesome sight on this new day seemed to me a brilliant symbol to sum up the miracle that God had done in my life that summer. The majestic, powerful Creator of the universe and the forces of nature that brought this Canyon into being had reached down from heaven to one of His suffering children. In the depths of my pain and despair and fear and doubt, He had resurrected a cherished dream and brought it to pass in the most unexpected and miraculous way. That's what He does best – not to immediately remove all of our struggles and suffering, but to work through them to bring us speechless before Him as His power works through our weaknesses.

From the Ends of the Earth

My chronically-ill physical body had been carried through a demanding summer of children's ministry and subsequent travel beyond what I ever could have hoped or imagined to do. Did He see my suffering? YES! Did He care? YES! Was my life useless or wasted because of what I could no longer do? NO WAY! God had proven Himself faithful every day of the previous four months, and had built into my life a testimony of His power and grace that would be in many ways a more amazing story than if He had snapped His fingers and given me instant healing as I had expected (and wanted) Him to.

After two weeks on the road, we drove back up the driveway to Geneva Hills. I had been part of this family holiday in every way, sharing in countless McDonald's meals, hundreds and hundreds of miles on the road, and family photos at various monuments. More than that, I had shared their lives and cemented what I hoped would be a lifelong friendship.

In the previous fortnight, I had learnt so much about American culture and history through the sites we had visited; I had learnt much more about God's love and faithfulness to me (even on holiday, my exhausted body needed His energy and grace to cope); and I had learnt and had shared so much of God's grace and generosity through this family of His faithful servants. But the story wasn't over yet!

With two weeks of my visa left, I was content to settle down at the house, doing very little. The children had started the new school year and I would be on my own for most of the days, free to sleep and rest.

Several days after our return from holiday, a Geneva Hills camp counsellor from past years dropped in. On his way back to Princeton Theological Seminary in New Jersey with a car loaded with belongings, Mark had stopped for a brief visit to John and Fay and the children.

Over lunch, Mark extended to me a friendly invitation to visit if I ever wanted to explore New Jersey and New York City; he would gladly show me around. The result of the conversation was the decision that there was no reason I couldn't go back with him right then for a few days.

Hastily tossing clothes and other necessities in my just-emptied backpack, I was about to embark on another road trip, this time going east through a part of West Virginia, the length of Pennsylvania and into New Jersey. Nine hours later, we arrived at the seminary.

During the next week, my own personal tour guide led me through another fabulous variety of travel experiences.

From the Ends of the Earth

From the casinos and Boardwalk of Atlantic City, to a barefoot stroll along the sand of a quiet beach as the waves crashed on the shore, I relished inhaling the salty sea air as sea gulls screeched overhead. After four months living in the Midwest, I felt 'at home' by the ocean once again. Not even a thought of swimming crossed my mind, however – not in the freezing Atlantic Ocean devoid of the tropical Pacific currents!

A couple of days later I was amid the frantic pace of New York City trying not to be so over-awed as to be run-over by fast-moving pedestrians or cars. Yes, I was really here at the Empire State Building, Macy's, Central Park and the Metropolitan Museum of Art. The view from the 107th floor of a World Trade Center tower was quite simply astonishing. Brisbane was a small country town in comparison to this megalopolis. A Broadway production of 'Miss Saigon' followed by fresh coffee and New York bagels with cream cheese ended a magnificent day which had made my head spin.

After a week away which included another day in New York City and some exploration of Princeton, I sat on a Greyhound bus headed back to Ohio. Waiting for others to board, I stared absently out the window watching the luggage being loaded into the bus compartments. My bright red backpack wasn't to be seen, but maybe it had been already stowed or was yet to come. However, when the bus driver boarded and started the engine and I still hadn't spotted my pack, I decided to follow through on a nagging insistence I was feeling.

Feeling faintly ridiculous, I nevertheless approached the driver and mentioned my luggage. Impatiently, he asked what it looked like and checked inside the bus station. Sure enough, there it was. With an inward sigh of relief and a prayer of thanks to the God who cares even about left-behind luggage, I seated myself again for the thirteen-hour journey through the night back to Columbus.

Finally it was time to leave Geneva Hills and my adopted summer family in a very emotional farewell.

As I was flying out of Los Angeles, I thought I might as well visit Disneyland before I went home, and so booked into the Fullerton Youth Hostel for a few nights. You know you're in California when there are earthquake instructions taped to the back of the dorm room doors! Nice to know, but I certainly hoped I wouldn't need them.

After making my acquaintance with Mickey and Minnie Mouse, adventuring with the Pirates of the Caribbean, and dizzying myself in the Mad Hatter's spinning teacups, one night in America remained on my itinerary. God had one more surprise in store to top off this trip.

One morning during breakfast at the hostel, I befriended a couple from Perth. As their flight was

From the Ends of the Earth

leaving the same day as mine, we decided to share the cost of a taxi to the airport. However, we discovered an Australian guy working at the hostel who had another little business on the side – he drove a limousine for hire and would happily take us to the airport for the cost of petrol.

It was an hilarious end to an amazing and miraculous trip – I had come to the USA with my backpack and fragile health to serve God, and in His faithfulness He had graced me with the energy I needed to last the summer, and an unbelievable travelogue of adventures that had spanned fourteen American states and even a little piece of Canada. I had seen some of the great American sights and yet I had not planned any of these adventures by my own efforts; indeed, God had not even given me more than a few days' advance warning for any of these trips. Now I was on my way to the airport – me and my backpack escorted in style in a stretch limo driven by an Australian!

I learned many spiritual lessons that summer, but two in particular stood out: Firstly – you cannot outgive God. I thought I was giving up a lot in terms of my health and finances to serve Him, but as I took a risk and gave Him what He asked for, He generously and faithfully gave me more than I ever could have imagined. His gifts and blessings often don't come in the form or at the time we expect, but they are usually more than we could have hoped for and of a more lasting kind.

I didn't receive healing from my illness, but God gave me instead grace and strength to do what He called me to do, and He gave me deeper faith to lean on Him and trust Him for my daily needs.

The second lesson is that God's timing is perfect....He is often not 'early' in our way of thinking, but He is never late. What we call 'last minute' is not actually that at all, as God is not bound by our understanding of time. As a human being (one who happens by nature to like to plan things far in advance with as much time to spare as possible), I would have called all of my post-camp travel experiences pretty 'last minute', but in reality, God presented me with each opportunity at the time I needed to know them, whether it was a week in advance, a day or even a couple of hours.

He knows what He's doing.

From the Ends of the Earth

Chapter 6

Back on Brisbane soil, reality hit brutally. My body now went into collapse mode as it desperately fought to regain the strength it had spent. It was very difficult not to feel despondent at times as the physical fatigue, pain and discomfort assailed my body. Once again I fought fear. Would I regress to where I was a year ago? Surely God wouldn't take me back to that? I could do nothing but rest as much as I could and ride it out for a while, trying to trust patiently in His good plans for my future.

A couple of months later, I was at the stage of job-hunting, although it was clear that I could not return to the legal profession in this state of health. In fact, looking for full-time work of any description was out of the question. However, while I was living with Mum and Dad I was not under great financial pressure so I planned to work part-time or casual hours for a year or so to get back on my feet properly, and return to full-time legal work after that. For now an income of some sort was the priority.

The obvious place to look for part-time or casual work was in the retail or administrative sector, and I began sending applications to local shops and businesses. I hadn't any previous retail experience, but plenty in the way of customer service and administrative skills. Frustratingly, time and time again I came up against the barrier of being 'over qualified'.

Time and time again I explained my health situation – sometimes I was met with understanding, sometimes with suspicion. One employer told me straight that he thought I would get bored too easily and he didn't want to go to the bother and expense of training me only to have me leave a month or so later. Willing to sign a year-long contract just so I could work, I felt at times that it would have been easier to stay on the dole, although this would have been not great for either the system or my psychological state.

A family friend recommended I approach our local library for a job. I hadn't seen any positions advertised, but sent in my resume regardless. Although our family had been avid local library clients when I was a child, since my later high school and university years I had hardly entered its doors. I had always loved books and libraries and maybe this was where my university job in the Law Library would help my cause.

At around this time, I also submitted a resume to a large local supermarket, and had been invited to an interview. To my delight, the manager took the view that my qualifications and desire to work would be an asset. After an informal interview and chat, he undertook to find me a position and phone me within the week. Excellent! After two months of unemployment, I now had a job for sure...or so I thought. One week went by, and then another and still I heard nothing. Another dead end.

A week after submitting my resume to the library, they too invited me to an interview, as two casual library assistant positions had arisen. I had a very positive interview and walked out fairly confident of a position. I was told that I would know by the Friday afternoon whether I had been successful, so all I had to do was wait a few days. Friday afternoon came and went, and the phone was silent. Disappointment again. 'C'mon, God – where *are* You?' was my frustrated cry at times, and yet I knew He had to have something in store for me. It was just the 'what' and 'when' that I didn't know.

Monday afternoon came, and to my surprise, the library phoned back with a job offer. They had been unable to phone me on Friday due to extenuating circumstances, and I accepted the job with no hesitation.

Just as the phone hit the cradle, it rang again. Unbelievably, it was the supermarket manager from several weeks earlier, also offering me a position. I thanked him for the offer, but told him that I had just accepted another position.

As I hung up the phone again, I felt a little shaken by the close timing of those two calls. My much preferred job was in the library, but what if the supermarket had phoned first? I would have accepted that job, assuming the library wasn't going to call. And why had the supermarket delayed a couple of weeks longer than they had said they would? I called it a pretty close shave, and wondered why, after a couple of months of job-hunting, God had allowed those two calls within seconds of each other.

There was that 'timing' lesson again. The closeness of the calls was not the real issue. God was in charge of the timing and order, and He had controlled those calls so that the one I was meant to receive first came first. A couple of seconds or minutes constituted a 'close shave' to me, but not to God.

As I was later to discover, it was crucial to God's plan for my life that I was to work in that library; not only for the following twelve months, as I had thought would be the case, but for eight years. It was the ideal place for all sorts of reasons that I wouldn't realise until later – for now, I was just glad to have a job and be receiving a wage.

I started my training at the library in December 1994, and even as I enjoyed the job and getting to know my colleagues, within me was still a strong pull towards the USA. Instead of quenching that thirst, as I thought my summer camp trip would do, my desire to return increased. To return to Geneva Hills the following summer I needed only a letter of invitation from my camp director and I kept the idea in the back on my mind.

I still had to use wisdom when considering my health, and I also knew that *my* desire to do something (even it if was a 'good thing' and in a Christian context) didn't necessarily mean that it was the *best* thing for me to do according to God's will for my life at that time. I couldn't just stick God's name on something and assume it was right. I had been provided with this good job, and I couldn't afford to toss it in lightly.

A couple more months went by, and after continuing to pray and think over the situation, I felt sure that returning to camp the following summer was the right thing to do. I submitted the appropriate paperwork, and began saving as hard as I could for the trip.

Strangely though, as another month passed and my health remained unstable, I felt a distinct lack of ease about the situation. Only working ten to twelve hours a week at the library my body was already emitting warning signs to be very careful not to push it too hard.

After a couple of weeks of inner turmoil, I decided that I couldn't go ahead with something about which I didn't have God's total peace. Although it was true that my health seemed at odds with the call to go the first time round, I had a very strong conviction that it was right. This time, I decided that the state of my body was in fact something God wanted me to pay close attention to. This was not the time to take a risky leap of faith. If I went ahead regardless, I couldn't blame Him for the consequences of something He hadn't wanted me to do in the first place. Reluctantly, I withdrew my camp application, and although my heart felt heavy about the decision, peace returned and I was at rest.

I don't know why I initially felt it was the right decision yet later knew it was not. Did I mishear God in the first place? It was entirely possible I had convinced myself that I was hearing God simply so I could justify something I wanted to do anyway. I found that issue a bit confusing and disturbing for a while.

Upon later reflection, I found assurance in pondering analogous situations. Saint Paul tells of plans to visit places he was later prevented from entering and I read of other missionaries having doors closed on opportunities they felt had been initially open to them – some were later saved from dangerous situations; some were guided to better opportunities; some never knew why they were led otherwise at late notice. Whatever the reason, I felt encouraged that I hadn't walked away from God or could no longer hear His voice clearly. My job wasn't to understand the 'whys', just to walk step by step in obedience according to His directions.

Settling well into my job at the library, I channelled my love for children into volunteering with Scripture Union. I was able to take the SU camp brochures into the library to put on the community notice board, and I soon gained a reputation for spending my work holiday time at camps with about forty primary school children. Some colleagues thought it was a noble thing to do, many probably thought I was just weird or crazy; but I didn't care. A five-day camp did tax my health, but God always enabled me to manage a week and go back to work after a weekend of sleep in between.

Strong friendships were being forged with a number of library staff, several of whom were around my own age. As it became known that I was a Christian, it was not uncommon to be asked questions about God and my faith, and sometimes lively discussions ensued with people of different spiritual backgrounds and beliefs.

I became particularly close to a fellow casual employee who commenced employment at the library only three weeks before I did. She had been on a journey of spiritual discovery – in her own words 'looking for something' but not knowing quite what or where to find it, just trying different things. Full of questions about God and Christianity, we would inevitably end up on this topic of conversation....not that we talked instead of working, I hasten to add!

Kathryn Kerridge

With two children at primary school, Leanne was also very interested in the Scripture Union camp brochures I took into the library four times a year; her daughter was old enough to attend and Leanne was keen to send her on the next camp I was going to – which happened to be in the September holidays. To my delight, she sent in the application form, and another library staff member decided to send her daughter along as well.

On the second night of camp, my group of six girls and I were all tucked up in our dorm beds. The 'lights out' command had been issued, but as the girls had been so quick getting into bed and quietening down, I allowed some whispered chatting. Almost immediately Leanne's daughter, who was sleeping on the top bunk above my bed, said, 'Kathryn, I'm not sure I'm going to heaven when I die, and I want to be sure.'

A Scripture Union camp involves a daily time of singing and Bible teaching in addition to the other fun activities of the holiday. During the week, a particular theme or portion of the Bible incorporates the basic gospel message of how our relationship with God was broken by sin, and the role of Jesus in mending that relationship through His death and resurrection. The choice of following Jesus and becoming a Christian is clearly presented during the week, and if children wish to respond further to that information, they are able to initiate conversation with a leader.

From the Ends of the Earth

Here we were on night two of camp – we hadn't even reached the stage of Bible teaching which mentioned heaven and what the Bible said about it. With a quick prayer for wisdom and the right words, I explained simply the gospel message and how to pray and ask God for forgiveness of our sins, and commit to following Jesus and obeying Him. Always very careful not to put pressure on a child to make this serious and life-changing commitment, I finished by giving her the option of praying to herself before she went to sleep that night; praying out loud so we could all hear; or continuing to think about this information during camp and afterwards so she could be sure this was what she wanted to do.

Without a moment's hesitation, my camper announced that she wanted to pray out loud, right then and there. As I lay on the bottom bunk in the darkness, hearing her become one of God's children, tears flowed silently from my eyes. As a Christian, it is an incredible privilege to introduce someone else to God, my best friend and my reason for being.

I felt God saying to me, as clearly as if He were whispering the words in my ear, 'If you had to suffer illness that made you leave your career and spend a year in bed, work casual hours in a library so that you could meet Leanne, to be on this camp with her daughter, and lead her to Christ – was it worth it?'

Without a doubt, I could say that it *was* worth it, and I would do it all again. My life was not just about me, but about God using it to help others. Often in order to do that He has to allow glitches/suffering/pain in our own lives so that we are ready and able to do so – this was a case in point.

On the heels of this understanding was the revelation that if I had gone back to the USA from June to September as I had planned, I would not even be here, and I was so thankful that I had heeded those inner warning bells that I believe were from God.

The following Monday when I returned to work, Leanne approached me to ask what I had done to her daughter who apparently was tidying her room, helping out at home, and had generally exhibited such a change in lifestyle and demeanour that her mother and father were a bit shell-shocked, but thrilled. Our friendship deepened, and as we enjoyed time together apart from work, our conversations inevitably centred on issues of God and faith.

Franklin Graham (son of renowned evangelist Billy) was scheduled to come to Brisbane in February the following year for a series of public meetings. My parents and I planned to attend, and were completing training sessions in order to be available to help people respond to the gospel message after the meetings. Before I had even had the chance to think about inviting Leanne along, she approached me at work, saying that she'd heard about the festival on the Christian radio station (96.5 FM), and was I going, because she would like to come along.

From the Ends of the Earth

A group of us attended the meeting at the Brisbane Exhibition grounds on a warm February evening, and enjoyed a picnic tea on the grass. At the end of his message, the speaker invited anyone who wanted to respond in some way to go to the front and speak with a volunteer. Leanne was one of the first on her feet, followed closely by her nine-year old son, and once again I felt God's assurance that although my life wasn't going anywhere near the track I had thought it would take, He made sure I was in the right place at the right time to accomplish His purposes.

The spiritual 'ripple effect' on this family continued over the next couple of years. Other family members and friends started going to church; a few became Christians themselves; and the two children came to more SU camps bringing friends along too. As far as the effect on my own life was concerned, I was seeing more and more of God's reasons for guiding my life the way He had been, and the faith that had been so shaken by the events of 1993-94 was growing stronger than ever. My understanding of God was infinitely broader, and I was more willing to let go of my own agenda and surrender to His plans instead of fighting them, as I trusted more in the goodness of His ways.

Although I had 'lost' a number of friends during my illness as our lives drifted apart, some of my existing friendships went to a deeper level.

A close friend from primary and high school became a Christian in our senior year at high school. However, after school our life paths took us in very different directions, and we gradually lost touch. She had gone through a very difficult few years personally, and eventually moved back to live with her parents as I had with mine. We were thus living only a couple of streets away from each other.

A couple of years after the worst of my illness was over, we re-established our friendship. Regular coffee and chats became part of our routine, and our lives drew closer than ever as we shared the struggles and frustrations of our different and yet similarly trying circumstances.

One afternoon, while having coffee at one of our favourite cafes, I was given an inkling of the difference my illness had made to our friendship. My friend explained that although she had loved and treasured our high school friendship and had respected my faith, she always felt that things had gone so easily for me – secure family, academic and sporting achievements, good relationships with friends and teachers, university entry, career – that I just couldn't really identify with the difficulties and issues of her life.

However, since going through my own personal trials, she felt that I really could understand what she was going through, and also that she could see my faith wasn't just something that I had because I had no problems to deal with. She was right – I did have a lot more compassion, understanding and empathy. The truth is that the world doesn't need to be preached at by Christians who have had an easy ride and have trite answers to all life's problems; the world needs Christians who have weathered pain and suffering and yet have experienced the comfort that hope in God brings. Once again, I was able to truly thank God for what He had allowed me to go through, not only for the changes it had triggered in my life, but also for the encouragement and help I was now able to pass on to others.

That is not to say I ceased to struggle with some of His ways in my life, and that I no longer cried out for answers when life was tough. I have a stubborn streak, and surrendering my will to God's when they clashed didn't occur without a fight on my part on occasion, I have to admit. The encouraging thing was that I could see myself changing for the better through all these times…although some days I wondered if there couldn't have been an easier way.

Chapter 7

My expectation was to be back at work full-time in the law after about a year of working casually in the library. However, as the months went by it soon became clear that wasn't going to happen. Twelve months on and my health was nowhere near good enough to even think of working full-time, let alone full-time in a profession which involved long hours and considerable pressure. I was going to have to learn to live longer term with this illness, and that took several years to come to grips with both physically and psychologically.

In the library, I averaged twelve to fifteen hours work a week for the first month. It didn't provide a lot of money, but was perfect for my health. Work took most of my physical energy; the rest of my time was largely spent resting or sleeping, with snatches of social time with friends.

A few months into the job, we became short-staffed and my hours increased to between twenty and thirty a week. At first, I coped with the extra hours but as the months continued, the drain on my body became more obvious and concerning. There had been talk of converting some casual jobs into permanent part-time positions. I would benefit greatly from a regular routine and eagerly awaited more information, but as the months went by and nothing definite eventuated, I wondered how long I would be able to keep going as a casual employee.

Finally, changes occurred and I obtained a job-share position. The regular hours – two days one week, three the next – led to a more stable state of health. My job-share partner and I worked together extremely well, and had the flexibility to swap our days around if necessary. The arrangement was a godsend and came at just the right time.

Our Young People's Library Service (YPLS) provided story clubs and storytelling sessions for playgroups and pre-schools as well as a fun school holiday programme four times a year. The holiday programme consisted of storytelling and craft for ages four to seven; craft for ages eight to ten; and craft for ages eleven to sixteen. To my delight, I was soon involved with one or two sessions each school holidays. The members of the YPLS team became good friends and willingly considered ideas that I had used successfully at SU camps.

The usual ME symptoms dogged me daily although they varied in degree. On a bad day it took focused energy and sheer force of will to do everything – sometimes it felt like hard work just to breathe, let alone get dressed and go to work; on a good day I felt more like my old self, able to enjoy life and people. I never quite knew what a day was going to be like – I could have a very 'bad' day for no apparent reason at all except that my body just decided it wouldn't work properly; sometimes a bad patch could be traced back to over-extending myself days or even weeks earlier. I could experience periods of weeks in length when life would consist merely of going to work and resting at home.

Still I fought frustration and impatience with my body and brain, and was so angry with this disease that robbed me of much enjoyment and achievement in life. I wasn't angry at God anymore, but often fell into the trap of relentlessly pushing my body to do what I wanted it to do, reasoning it was good that I was 'fighting' the illness. I would *not* let it beat me! Patches of relatively 'good' health became a danger time as I tried to catch up on what I had been missing and pretend I was normal. Eventually my body would reach its limit and crash to rock bottom again.

In despair, Mum tried to encourage me to see that trying to fight the illness this way was only destructive. To accept the way things were and work with what I had would be more likely to lead to a better quality of life.

Stubbornly I persisted, until I became thoroughly sick of the rollercoaster ride – swinging wildly from weeks in bed to maniacally using up all the energy I had saved, and then landing in bed again for weeks feeling weak and horrible, paying dearly for a few days of normal living. Only in accepting my limitations and taking care of my body and its needs would it serve me more reliably and less painfully in the longer term.

I figured I was probably able to live life at about fifty percent of what it was before, so if that meant working half that time, it would also mean at least halving everything else...socialising, physical activity, volunteering. I learnt to look more sensibly at my plans over a week or fortnight at a time. My energy levels were a bit like my fortnightly wage – there was a fixed amount which I could spend as quickly or slowly as I chose – it could be used up in the first couple of days and make me 'bankrupt' the rest of the time or be spent gradually. Prioritising what was most important to me was the key. Work commitments had to be fulfilled regardless, so if I was going through a bad patch and all my energy was used up at work, well, I just had to live with that.

Difficult as it was to accept my limitations, the quality of my life improved greatly, and I realised this was how I would 'win' against the disease – not by ruthlessly punishing my body, but by being kind to it and listening to the signals I was given.

Psychologically, the battle continued as I fought feeling lazy ('only' working part-time and spending so much time in bed), unreliable (I would often have to pull out of social events at the last minute if my body 'hit the wall'), and stupid (I hated forgetting things, mixing up my words, losing my train of thought and not being able to process information quickly – Good grief! I was supposed to be an articulate lawyer by this stage of my life). I had to constantly remind myself that my value was not based on what I could do but rather in who I was, and I had nothing to prove to anyone.

The lack of momentum in my life was frustrating as I moved from my mid- to late twenties. Most of my friends were now married and starting to have children; most had established careers, travelled, purchased houses…all the stuff you were 'supposed' to be doing at that stage of life. I seemed to be merely marking time in comparison, not doing any of those things or even able to make future plans to do them.

I had an enormous amount to be thankful for – loving parents who were happy for me to continue living at home and contribute to the expenses of using their house and car; an enjoyable job which paid more than the minimum wage and had good working conditions; and a more stable state of health than many other ME sufferers had.

Staying centred on God was vital to avoid the trap of comparing my life with that of others, or of being achievement-driven as my nature was inclined. That path only led to frustration, resentment and depression (I know; I walked it too many times), and would cause me to overlook all the blessings God had given me, and all the things I was still able to do.

Emotionally and socially ME affected how much social interaction I could cope with. My body didn't distinguish between energy used for work or play, so if I used up all my week's energy at work and there was none for social engagements, that was that. My body didn't re-energise by playing sport, going to the movies or having a phone conversation with a friend – all interaction and activity sapped me to some extent. Consequently many times I just didn't have the strength to meet up with a friend or even have a phone conversation although I was starving for social contact. On a bad day, the sound of voices and laughter was harsh noise with which I was unable to cope, and I could be so exhausted that the thought of having to string words into sentences and interact in conversation was more than I could bear.

Loneliness was a common sensation, not only when I was actually on my own, but because even when I was with people there was a sense in which my whole lifestyle was so unlike the norm that I felt isolated. Like existing inside an invisible glass bubble, I was 'in' the real world – I had a job; I had friends; I was able to do things – but I couldn't get fully involved with life. My family and close friends included and accepted me as I was, but blank looks or misunderstanding emerged if I had to explain my behaviour or lifestyle to others. It did hurt to know that some people thought I was just malingering or lazy or undisciplined, but I had to grow a tougher skin and not care so much about people's perceptions of me. Becoming defensive and trying to explain or justify myself only used up precious energy anyway. Boiled down, the source of the struggle was pride – not wanting others to think badly of me – and the misplaced desire for approval that had been evident since I was a child.

Because my relationship with God had deepened so much during my months of being bedridden, I had learned to lean on Him, and although I was lonely, I knew I was never alone. After all, Jesus had lived in the world in a human body and He knew what it felt like to be exhausted, misunderstood and lonely. My tears and frustrations were poured out to God in the knowledge that He saw every single one and cared deeply enough to listen. He also cared deeply enough not to let that be the end of it, and continued to reveal areas in my life where my character needed refining and my reactions to circumstances and situations needed to change.

There were so many children who would give anything for the love and care and stability that I had received from my parents as I grew up. Only as I grew older did I fully appreciate all their love, work and sacrifices over my lifetime. However, although I loved them very much and knew that I was very blessed to have a loving home in which to stay, my relationship with my parents went through some difficult patches as I struggled to cope with my lifestyle restrictions.

From the Ends of the Earth

Because of the size and layout of my parents' two-storey home, I was able to live in a kind of 'granny flat' on the ground floor next to the garage. I had spent my sickest year in a bedroom upstairs where Mum could help nurse me, and where I was near the bathroom and kitchen (downstairs there was a toilet, but no bathroom or kitchen). When my brother left home to work overseas, moving downstairs gave me more independent living, and I could shut myself away in a quiet space when I needed to.

In my late twenties, as I succumbed to the frustration of my life 'marking time', I also retreated more and more from Mum and Dad. Internally I raged that I shouldn't still have to be living at home at my age, when I dearly wanted to buy a place of my own and have a 'normal' life.

Burdening my mind, too, was the thought that my parents had worked so hard all their lives to provide for my brother and me, and it wasn't fair that they were still landed with me at twenty-five, twenty-six, twenty-seven, twenty-eight... I was keenly aware that I wasn't earning enough to live independently and I needed the use of their house, electricity, hot water, and car.

Dad often reassured me that it made no difference to them that I was still at home – they certainly weren't pressuring me to move out, or making me feel as though I wasn't paying my way (only *I* was making me feel like that). Although I knew and appreciated this, I wanted to be independent from my parents by now – after all, they knew far more about me and my comings and goings than parents normally would of their adult daughters, even though Mum and Dad weren't at all nosy.

I didn't always deal well with this internal struggle, especially when combined with any ME relapses I suffered, when pain and exhaustion blew everything out of perspective and impaired my ability to cope with life in general. Frustration all too often manifested itself in snapping at Mum and Dad, or shutting them out of my life with minimal interaction. I knew this was hurtful, but felt unable to cope in any other way, and then felt awful about that, when I knew they would have done just about anything to find a cure for my illness. To their eternal credit, Mum and Dad had endless patience with me, never stopped loving me, and never stopped telling me that they loved me despite my behaviour – talk about an incredible example of unconditional love.

Needless to say, God revealed this as a *big* area to work on in terms of my character. There was no excuse for taking my frustrations out on *anyone*, much less on my loving and supportive family; no amount of pain or exhaustion justified that kind of bitter behaviour. The emotions of anger, frustration and grief that inevitably arose had to be dealt with maturely lest I become bitter and resentful and 'prickly' because I had let life's circumstances make me hard and cold. There was always, always, *always*

From the Ends of the Earth

a choice between reacting like this or the response of allowing these trials to make me sweeter and more Christ-like in character. I had to learn not to be so impulsive and explosive, reacting out of pure emotion (another trait I had manifested since childhood), and to cultivate a lot more self-control.

I am pleased to say that God has done wonderful things to strengthen my relationship with my parents over the years and we are now as close as we could possibly be! I thank God for them every day - they are my heroes and I honour them and love them more than words can say. I have required their forgiveness many times and they have graciously given it time and time again. Mum and Dad, I love you!

Kathryn Kerridge

Chapter 8

My passion for working with children burned as brightly as ever and I loved attending Scripture Union primary camps once or twice each year. I sometimes volunteered in the Brisbane office of SU and for seven years visited a Christmas/New Year beach mission to run a bush dance. I knew that God was enabling me to share my faith with others at work, at camps, and with my friends, but still I struggled with the thought that I couldn't 'be' where every other person my age was at in this usual stage of life – would I *ever* own my own home, or even a car, or be married, have children or have the career for which I had spent five years at university?

The library was a good workplace for me – I loved books and I loved people and I enjoyed the interaction with other staff and regular library clients (especially the children). Besides, mountains of brand-new books and magazines were at my disposal for borrowing. However, I could do a good day's work without being greatly mentally challenged. Although I knew I was capable of more, further study to be a librarian or a library technician was necessary to advance in the field. Realistically I could only do one thing part-time; study *or* work. I couldn't afford not to work, so that was the answer.

From the Ends of the Earth

Returning to the legal profession with its long hours, stress and need for mental clarity at all times was not an option, and as more years passed since my graduation, all those years of study seemed rather a waste, even though I knew God must have had *some* purpose in it. In truth, the bigger picture revealed that obtaining my degrees was maybe less about the book learning and knowledge of the law than it was about the personal and spiritual development God had accomplished in me. What a contrast between the shy teenager who entered university and the more confident, wise and bold twenty-two year old who walked out five years later. However, even though my brain wasn't up to doing what it used to do, I often longed for it to be more stretched and challenged.

Occasionally I scoured the newspaper's employment pages, wondering what other options I had for part-time work. I still desired to work with children, and as teacher-training wasn't an option for me at this point, I considered teacher aide positions.

During one personally frustrating period in 1996, about five teacher aide positions were advertised in a single edition of our local paper. Determined to make a change from the library (I had told God I just *had* to move on), I submitted applications for all of them. Adding to my experience and skills with children my computer and administrative skills from various jobs, I had no problems at all addressing each of the selection criteria, and I was certain that one of those jobs would be mine. Imagine my bewilderment when I was not called for even a single interview for any of those positions. How could this be?

Wrestling with this turn of events, I had to smile wryly at the mental image of God gently but firmly keeping His hand on my head to stay in His will for me in the library, even though I kept trying to wriggle away. The message was clear – I was exactly where He wanted me to be, and I must make peace with that and Him, and submit to His will even though I thought I knew better.

At one point during these years, I remember quite clearly a conversation with God during which I asked, 'When are you going to heal me?' I hadn't received any direct revelation from Him that He *would* actually heal me on this earth, but I still hoped and prayed that He would, and knew that He *could*. For some reason this day my mind posed the question not as an 'If' but a 'When'. A phrase came directly to my mind in answer, and I knew it was God – 'When the most glory will go to Me!'

How bizarre, I thought – 'That doesn't make sense, Lord. You could heal me *anytime* and glory would go to You! The miracle would be evident to everyone who knows me, and I would certainly attribute it to Your power. You could have healed me way back at the time of summer camp in the USA and glory would have gone to You.'

From the Ends of the Earth

The answer came back again, clear as a bell, 'No, you're not listening! I said, "When the *most* glory will go to Me!"' I still couldn't really figure that out, but God gave me understanding a short time later.

One day I was reading from my Bible John chapter 11, which gives the account of Jesus raising his friend Lazarus from the dead. The passage brought light to my mind about what God had been doing with my circumstances and life, and why His recent comment to me actually wasn't as bizarre as it sounded.

Jesus had been told by a messenger that his friend was sick – Lazarus' sisters, Mary and Martha, had sent for Jesus in desperation, knowing that if anyone could heal him, He could. Jesus' reply was, '*This sickness will not end in death. No, it is for God's glory…*' (*John 11:4 NIV*). The next two verses reveal a perplexing paradox – the first says that Jesus loved Lazarus and his two sisters; the next says 'yet He stayed where He was two more days'.

No doubt Mary and Martha couldn't believe it – they had trusted Jesus could help, called on Him in faith, knew that He loved them…and yet He not only didn't hurry to help them, He didn't do anything at all for a while – and yet He had said glory would go to Him in the situation. Hmmm, sound familiar?! Oh yes, there had been many times I had tried to figure that course of action out.

Finally, Jesus went to visit his friends, and His disciples decided to go with Him to see what would happen. Mary and Martha's words to Jesus revealed that they, too, struggled with His actions (or lack thereof) – like me, they loved Jesus, believed He was God's Son and had power to heal, and yet wondered why He hadn't intervened to heal when He so easily could have.

The Bible says that when Jesus saw their sorrow, He was deeply moved. Verse 35, the shortest in the Bible, says simply *'Jesus wept.'* (NIV) He was not hardened, callous, and indifferent either to the pain of his friends, or to the loss of His own friend's life. His lack of action at the expected time did not in any way reveal a lack of love; it just revealed purposes higher than what human eyes could understand. It had been a long road for me to get to this point of understanding, but this I knew with certainty was the truth.

The story concludes with Jesus going to the tomb and asking for it to be opened. By this stage, Lazarus had been dead four days. What on earth could Jesus be intending to do at this late stage? By this point, there was quite a crowd gathered around...family members, Jesus' disciples, Jewish mourners and no doubt a bunch of curious hangers-on who had gathered during the walk to the tomb.

Jesus prayed, reiterating that this whole chain of events was designed to bring glory to God and to reaffirm that He Himself was God's Son, and called Lazarus out of the tomb. In what must have been quite a comical scene, the dead man walked out (or more likely hopped out), still bound with the strips of grave clothes and a cloth around his face! No doubt the crowd was absolutely astonished.

Could Jesus have performed a miracle earlier? Yes. Would glory have gone to God? Yes. Why didn't He act when people thought He should have? Because He had a much bigger purpose in mind; one which would test the faith of those involved and one which would be far more dramatic and reach a wider audience; all because He knew this was the point at which 'the *most* glory would go to Him'.

This story wasn't an absolute assurance from God that He would totally heal *my* body in this lifetime – maybe He will, maybe I will have to wait until I get my perfect body in heaven where no sickness or pain can blight it ever again. The point for me was reassurance that God loves and cares for me no less because He was allowing me to live with an illness and its limitations – He weeps when I weep and feels my pain. It is absolutely right and proper that I continue to affirm my faith in Him and believe that He can work miracles; it is just not up to me to decide or command if and when they should occur.

I was reminded that God has a much bigger purpose and sometimes a bigger audience in store to which to display His power. His plans far outweigh mine.

Kathryn Kerridge

Chapter 9

My work in the library and ever-increasing involvement with YPLS continued. My health could now cope with a little more than my library hours so I began working with the Council's Outside School Hours Care programme at local primary schools. I loved working with the children; making their breakfast or afternoon tea, helping with homework, playing games and doing crafts with them for a couple of hours before or after school.

My annual leave entitlement was accruing. Some I used for SU camps, but I couldn't see the point of using the rest of my holiday leave to 'chill out' at home, pottering and reading or gardening etc. For anyone with a 'normal' life, that might be a heavenly thought, but I spent too much of my time doing that kind of stuff already, so it seemed to me like a bit of a waste. Why not save the time up for 'something big', although I had no particular idea of what or when that might be. At the very least I hoped at some point to go back to the USA to visit friends.

In all these years after my first summer in America, my passion for the country had not shrivelled with time or with my advancing age. I kept in touch by email and letters with John and Fay, a few other summer staff, and a number of my campers.

From the Ends of the Earth

At the beginning of each year I requested of God a return to America for summer camp but each time, the answer was a no. Although disappointed, I trusted that God had my best interests at heart, and that if He wanted me to stay in Australia, then that was the best place for me. Quite possibly, that first visit to the States was only ever meant to be a 'one-off thing' in His plan. I was willing to accept that, but couldn't understand why my desire for the country and camp ministry there didn't abate with time if that was the case. At times, I even felt what was like homesickness for the USA. Very weird, especially since I had only actually spent four months in the country – how can you be homesick from that?

There was no lack of Australian children with which to be involved and Scripture Union camps for primary-aged children became the highlights of my year. My gifts were also applied in other capacities with SU Queensland as God opened doors I never expected - serving on the Primary Camping Committee, teaching modules of SU's Children's Ministry Course and leading electives such as 'Arts and Crafts for Primaries' at SU's annual Christian Workers' Training Day. A surprise treat was having my airfare to Cairns paid for so I could lead the Bible teaching times at a day camp on the Atherton Tableland.

Although I couldn't figure out where my 'upside-down' life was heading, God ensured that I was plentifully supplied with children's ministry

Kathryn Kerridge

opportunities and there was no doubt that He was orchestrating the events of my life.

While I was at it, I thought I may as well include Mum and Dad in the SU camp experience. Sunday School teachers and youth group leaders since they were married, their commitment to church youth and children's ministry continued year after year, no matter how few other people joined them in their work. They loved children, and the children loved them.

SU Queensland valued having Christian couples on primary camps, not to have any particular leadership responsibilities as a group leader does, but just to 'be there' as extra adults for whatever they felt able to do – whether that be helping in the kitchen or looking after any ill or homesick children – and to be a positive model of marriage and family life.

Most 'camp parents' were couples with young children, but I managed to convince Mum and Dad that age wasn't a barrier – they had the Christian commitment, strong marriage, and loads of love and talents we needed. Who cared if they were a bit older? There was always room for camp grandparents!

It was so much fun for me to watch my Mum and Dad in action with the children, just being themselves. With a special table in the dining room, a different small group would be issued a coveted

From the Ends of the Earth

invitation to join them at each meal. The table was laden with special goodies…party decorations, candles, soft drink, bowls of lollies and nuts, special desserts, sparklers and party poppers. The final night's invitation belonged to the leaders who gathered at Camp Mum and Dad's table for some well-deserved pampering.

Some of the most touching memories of all my SU camping years involve my Mum and Dad – as they sat on the grass in the sun with a camper who had hurt himself and couldn't play the running game; judging dorm inspections when Camp Mum was 'bribed' by the campers with chocolates and flowers for the highest score; walking along the beach and hearing a girl who had lived in various foster homes for seven years say, 'Camp Dad, can I walk with you?'; and seeing another girl from a very traumatic family background saying, 'Camp Dad, you sit down and rest, and I'll massage your feet. I'm good at that.' The week would be peppered with children's voices calling for 'Camp Mum' or 'Camp Dad' to help them, to sit next to them, be on their team for something, or just to talk to them. Just goes to show you're never too old to go on an SU camp.

At this time I joined Mum and Dad in the Sunday School ministry at the Presbyterian Church in which I grew up and which my parents had continued to attend.

Kathryn Kerridge

For a number of years during my early years of illness, my church attendance was very sporadic. Obviously I didn't go at all when I was really ill, and when I returned from my trip to the USA and started work, there were many Sundays spent in bed in order to have enough energy to work the following week. Some Sundays I could have assimilated the sermon but was too exhausted to sit upright and interact with people afterwards.

Still, my spiritual growth was a priority, and my 'food' came from my Bible tapes and Christian sermons on television and radio. I did miss the sense of being part of a church family, but my Christian friends continued to be a source of spiritual strength and fellowship – God was enabling me to 'do' church in a different way for a while. Eventually my health stabilised to the point where I could be at church at least every second week, and I attended a local church with a cousin who had recently become a Christian.

In the late 1990s it became clear that my mum would soon require a hip replacement operation. She had suffered from osteoarthritis for many years, but the doctors had delayed an operation for as long as possible due to her relatively young age. The time had come when she was losing her footing more and more and was in constant pain, so hip replacement surgery was scheduled for early 1999.

From the Ends of the Earth

Post-operation, Mum would not be allowed to bear weight on that leg for three months. Among the many other lifestyle adjustments during her recovery, her Sunday School involvement would have to cease.

Dad couldn't lead the group on his own and I became certain that God was prompting me to go back to Mum and Dad's church to work alongside Dad and keep the Sunday School going. My parents were delighted, not only because the ministry could continue for the children, but because they had been longing for some 'new blood' and youth in leadership, fearing they were losing touch with the kids because of their age. I didn't think they needed to worry about that – God was clearly using all the abilities and love they were giving, but it was about time for a 'revamp' of the programme.

Sunday School was renamed 'KidZone' and I painted a big bright sign to display outside the church building on Sunday morning. With my guitar in hand, I led the singing time, introducing contemporary camp songs that I taught Mum and Dad as we went along. Initially the children were divided into two age groups for small group times.

Six months later, numbers had risen from an average of about six to around twenty children, and God answered our prayers for more volunteers to help. Mum was back on her feet in six months, mobile and pain-free, to complete our team.

1999 was the year Mum received a new hip… KidZone started at church…and the momentum of my life suddenly started to speed up – but as usual, not in the way I expected.

From the Ends of the Earth

Chapter 10

January 1999 - I was now twenty-eight years old, still working part-time in the library, still living with ME, still living at home, still single, and still feeling, lifestyle-wise, a million miles away from most of my other friends. I was thankful to God for the continued stability of my health, a good job, and the ministry opportunities I had been able to pursue. However, this strong internal pull towards camp ministry in the USA remained. Another new year...but the same old question was posed of God – 'May I go back to America?'

This year, the answer would set in motion a chain of events that would take me in a very different direction over the next decade of my life. And all this time I had been worried that my life was stagnating and going at such a snail's pace that I was being left behind. Little did I know....

One Sunday morning in early January, I was sitting alone at a table at the local McDonald's. I had visited a friend's church awaiting Mum and Dad to collect me on the way home from their church service. Sitting in the shade with a cold drink on a searing Brisbane summer's day, I pondered the year ahead of me and asked God if He could please send me back to the USA *this* year?....or at least could I go *somewhere* outside of Brisbane to do some children's ministry? I just wanted something a bit different to look forward to. Oh well, I thought, if all else fails, maybe I could use my savings to finally buy a car– I would settle for that as a goal.

God's one-word answer was immediate and startling – 'Romania'.

Unexpected it may have been, but it wasn't *totally* random. Immediately a train of thought opened up in my mind. For the previous nine years I had been sponsoring a little girl in a Romanian children's home through a Christian organisation called Mission Without Borders (MWB).

My first sponsor child was named Aurelia, but after she was taken out of her orphanage, another little girl, Florentina (Florrie for short), was allocated to me. I was able to write letters and send her packages and in turn, I received an annual photo and school update as well as little cards with drawings and translated messages, which I treasured.

Of the extensive ministry and relief work of MWB in the former communist countries of Romania, Moldova, Ukraine, Bulgaria, Albania and Bosnia, my heart was touched most by the summer camp programme for children from the homes. Through this programme, deprived and often unloved and abandoned children enjoyed a week of nutritious and abundant food, fresh air, games, friendship and stories from the Bible.

From the Ends of the Earth

Several years previously, I had received a surprise phone call from the then-Australasian director of MWB. Based in New Zealand, he was visiting the Australian office and was phoning long-time supporters to thank and encourage them. Touched, I enjoyed a lovely chat with him, but since then we had no further personal contact.

As these initial thoughts began swirling round my brain, Mum and Dad arrived to pick me up. On the short drive home, I mentioned my hunch that God might be calling me to go to Romania but I had no idea when or how. While my comment was no doubt rather a surprise, Mum and Dad didn't think I was completely out of my mind. They simply listened to my thoughts, as they had back in 1994, and set themselves to pray as I sought God's will on the matter.

The next day, I emailed the MWB director in New Zealand, asking about volunteering in Romania. His reply both stunned me and confirmed to me that I really was hearing God's voice in the McDonald's parking lot that Sunday, and not making up something in my head!

The international office of MWB in Los Angeles had decided only a few months previously to trial a volunteer mission trip to Romania this year. The programme would predominantly consist of assisting at a summer camp for children from homes supported by MWB. The director would be happy to endorse me as an Australasian candidate. At that point only a draft application form was available and I filled it out immediately. The application process resulted in a team of four, including myself, who would visit Romania for two weeks in the coming August. God obviously answered my prayers with a 'no' to America, but a definite 'yes' to another overseas opportunity which included the possibility of meeting Florentina.

The next step was applying for holidays from my job. My accumulated annual leave by this time totalled three months. Since the journey to Europe from Australia was so long, and the airfare costs substantial, why not take all of my holiday time and make a decent trip of it?

What I didn't realise was that I wasn't supposed to accumulate my annual leave at all. The staffing and financial reasons made perfect sense to me when explained by my boss...only no one had ever specified this to me until now. No way could I use all my annual leave for this trip. Willing to negotiate around certain dates, my boss approved eight weeks of my leave, the rest to be taken later but before the end of the next financial year.

Now I had two months of travel to plan. Return airline tickets between Brisbane-London and London-Bucharest were arranged first. A Romanian visa could be purchased upon arrival at the airport. For the short time remaining to travel in the UK and one or two European countries, visas were unnecessary so that was one less thing to organise.

Something kept nagging at me, though. My brother had been nursing in London for a few years, first on a working holiday visa and then using a 'Certificate of Entitlement to the Right of Abode' for the UK. Both he and I were entitled to this because of Mum's British birth; in effect it enabled us to live and work in the UK and go back and forth between Australia and the UK as we wished.

Great as this was, it was not required of me at the time. I hardly had the health to live and work and travel overseas for a year or two as my brother was doing; neither did I have the sort of qualifications which would enable me to earn a lucrative income there, nor a career to advance with overseas experience, as was the situation with Andrew. Besides, the right of abode cost hundreds of dollars; just going to Europe for my two weeks in Romania was going to cost several thousand dollars, and I wasn't looking for unnecessary ways to spend money.

OK, so I didn't *have* to get a right of abode in my passport but that niggling feeling wouldn't leave me. Oh well, I thought, I may as well go ahead with it – once I have this thing in my passport, it's done, and one day it might be possible to work in the UK for a few months to make it worthwhile. I might as well make the most of Mum's British birth since not everyone had this privilege.

Kathryn Kerridge

My Australian passport was thus stamped with a Certificate of Entitlement to the Right of Abode. One immediate advantage was that upon arrival in the UK after my two-day journey, I could quickly pass through immigration with British passport-holders instead of waiting with all the other internationals in the longer lines. That had to be considered a bonus after the arduous (and no doubt, fairly sleepless) flights.

Paperwork sorted, an itinerary to fill in my eight week trip was the next step. A blank calendar was drawn up and I went to work filling the days. First to go in were my Romania dates – that was the easy bit.

My brother was still working in London, so I figured on spending some time there on arrival while I recovered from jet lag, so I pencilled in that week. Next I added a week in Paris to finally make some use of my seven and a half years of French language study through high school and university. (My high school French teacher would be rather unimpressed if I went so close to France without actually visiting!) There were dozens of other places I could possibly visit, but during my planning I realised that although I wanted to travel and see places, I wanted to spend more than two weeks doing some sort of Christian ministry with children. What I really wanted was another mission opportunity. What else could I do that would be fairly simple to organise at this stage?

I had ten years of service with Scripture Union, so that was the obvious international organisation to which to turn my attention. As I was flying in and out of London anyway, and Andrew was living there…surely I could do a camp or beach mission with SU in England.

As it turned out, the head of primary work in SU Queensland had recently travelled to the UK and Europe, spending some time with several staff of Scripture Union in Scotland. One had subsequently made a reciprocal visit to Brisbane, and I was given his name as a contact.

Scotland hadn't been considered in my planning, but I emailed my contact, asking if there was anything I could be involved with either side of my trip to Romania. An SU Scotland holiday camp booklet was sent to me, and I went to work selecting a camp out of the dozens listed.

I definitely wanted a camp for primary school children, and only one fit around the dates of my fixed travel plans. It would be held at a site called Lendrick Muir in central Scotland, after I returned from Romania. I sent off my volunteer application form and waited for the outcome of my form and references. I heard nothing for some time and almost resigned myself to the fact that this plan wasn't going to work out. On my last day of work before the trip, a final check of my email at about 3.30pm revealed a message from SU Scotland of acceptance on that camp team. Just in time, one would think…although my understanding of time in God's sense had changed quite a lot over the years. As usual, He had ensured I had all the information I needed just when I needed it.

The following day, June 24, I checked in my trusty backpack at the airport and boarded my flight to London. In January I had prayed for 'something exciting' to do this year and now I was on my way. What I didn't realise was that I had just spent my last full year in Australia for at least the next decade.

I spent my first few days in Britain on a road trip with my brother. Andrew had hired a car for the weekend and as he settled himself behind the wheel, he handed me a giant road atlas of Britain. Apparently it was now my job to navigate. I don't have a good sense of direction at the best of times, let alone in a foreign country after a sleepless couple of days in flight to the other side of the world!

We managed to cover an enormous list of places in a couple of days. Still jetlagged and a little dazed, I was now seeing famous places and landmarks one after the other….Brighton (only the British could call an expanse of pebbles and stones near the ocean a 'beach'), Stonehenge, Bath (ah, all those Jane Austen novels I loved), the Cotswolds, Nottingham, Oxford, Cambridge, Windsor and Stratford-upon-Avon. The sheer age of the castles, cathedrals, and cobbled streets overwhelmed me. Back home, if a building

From the Ends of the Earth

was 100 years old, it was considered positively ancient! This really was history come alive to me, and I soaked it all in, even though I was so weary it all seemed like a bit of a blur.

After our weekend of travels, London beckoned. Andrew had booked me into a hostel/hotel in Bayswater for a week, and as we neared the city, he told me quite nonchalantly that I would have to direct him as he'd never driven into the city of London before. What? I've been in the country three days and you want me to navigate you through this city of *seven million* people, with about fifteen lanes of traffic on the motorway into the city?!!! Andrew's reply? 'Come on, people do this every day, so it can't be that bad!' Yeah, right. We had to go round a few blocks a few times to find the right turnoffs, but we finally made it. I discovered later that Andrew had quite a job getting back out of the city...no doubt because I wasn't sitting next to him sharing my expert navigational skills. Ha!

The next week while Andrew was back at work, I pounded the pavements of London to all the usual tourist haunts – the changing of the guard at Buckingham Palace, Westminster Abbey, the Tower of London, Madame Tussaud's Wax Museum, Hyde Park, Kensington Palace, Oxford St, Downing St, the Houses of Parliament, Covent Garden, a couple of musicals in the West End... I walked miles each day and by the end of the week must have looked as if I knew my way around as other tourists sometimes stopped to ask me for directions; to my surprise I was often able to help!

Also on the agenda were plans for my trip to Paris the following week. Booking a ticket on the Eurostar train was no problem. Organising accommodation, however, proved a little trickier. By nature, I liked to have all the details confirmed well ahead of time, and didn't feel so comfortable 'winging it' in strange situations. Consequently, my plan was to book a hostel room in Paris from London so I was assured of a bed to sleep in and only had to find the place when I arrived.

However, things were not to be so simple. My journal reveals my desire to be stretched by God in new experiences I would face travelling solo and He certainly took me at my word. The old adage comes to mind, 'Be careful what you pray for...you might just get it!'

Working through the youth hostel listings in my travel guides, I discovered that most would accept only a small number of advance bookings so the bulk of accommodation was available for those that turned up on the day. Every single hostel I called gave me the same answer – no bookings available and I should just phone the hostel when I arrived in Paris. At the time, this made me very uncomfortable. Peak tourist season in Paris and travelling on my own – what if I couldn't find an affordable place to stay? I had visions of having to sleep in the train station in a worst case scenario!

I had the name of a hostel miles outside the city centre which at least took a 'temporary' booking from me for a room. I didn't really want to stay so far out of the city but this gave me a backup accommodation plan. Better than nothing, I supposed. I would just have to wait and see what transpired when I arrived in Paris.

God was obviously teaching me how to be flexible instead of the rigid control freak that I tended to be, and how to be unfazed and at peace in the face of problems or inconveniences – not something I was naturally disposed to. Well so far I had had a plethora of opportunities to learn and change! Without the ability to relax and deal calmly with unexpected situations, I would never cope with many of the circumstances that would arise in subsequent years.

On July 2, I was in the Eurostar lounge of the 'international' train station. I found this somewhat amusing, as of course there is no such thing in Australia. The train headed off to France via the 'Chunnel' under the English Channel. On the French side I was greeted with scenes of the beautiful countryside, and three hours after leaving London I arrived in Paris and disembarked at the Gare du Nord.

Kathryn Kerridge

After seven years of French study, even allowing for a time lapse of seven years since, I expected to be able to understand what was going on around me, grasp instructions and words from people's conversations, and impress them with my language skills. In complete contrast, I actually found it confusing, noisy, and definitely out of my comfort zone. To quote from my journal that day - 'Did I say it felt GOOD to be stretched? What was I thinking? I've spent most of the afternoon feeling nothing short of freaked out!!!' As you can see, I was clearly *not* a confident solo traveller at that point.

The first hurdle was accommodation. I phoned through my listings of city hostels but as I had feared, every single one I tried was full. Panic welled up within, even though I knew I was being irrational; fatigue and disorientation was clouding my perspective.

I resorted to the hostel for which I had a temporary booking. It was completely off my map of Paris, but at least it was a room. The person on the phone spoke only French, and his speech was so fast that I wasn't able to understand any of the directions but the name of the train station at which to disembark. Requesting a slow repeat of his instructions was no help. Armed with the name of the station, help came in the form of a friendly attendant at the information centre, who not only gave me a metro map but wrote down the train times, lines, and changes necessary to get to Athis Mons. I could have hugged her!

From the Ends of the Earth

At Athis Mons, I hauled myself up a very steep hill to the hostel and was soon seated on a bed in a four bunk en-suite dorm. A very long and very hot shower revitalised my body and my spirits. A little later, the first of my roommates appeared. Mary was a teenage French girl from the country who was in Paris for a week and delighted that she could practice her English with me. Ah, ease of communication again!

The hassles and fatigue of the past eight hours started to melt away, and I was soon basking in the warm sunshine in the hostel front yard, chatting to some other Aussies and a family of Canadians. Excitement returned with the prospect of exploring Paris the following day.

For the next week, in stunningly bright and hot summer sunshine (unlike the English weather I had experienced thus far), I roamed the city and explored Notre Dame, the Eiffel Tower, the Sacre Coeur Basilica, the Louvre and other art galleries, strolling over the many bridges of the River Seine. Memories of high school French classes with our highly enthusiastic French teacher frequently brought a smile to my face. On the front cover of our senior French textbook was a large photo of the bizarrely-designed Georges Pompidou Centre. How surreal to be now surveying it in real life. I found it somewhat amusing that I was now buying metro tickets using exactly the same conversations we had practised in class at school.

Kathryn Kerridge

After a full first day of sightseeing, I caught the train back to the hostel. Although not the convenient city centre accommodation I had envisioned for myself, I was to discover that God had a couple of specific reasons for my being there.

The first was a Parisian man in his fifties. Patrick was obviously a local resident and friend of the hostel owners, and was often found sitting in the hostel garden chatting with other staff or guests.

Patrick spoke limited English, and when he discovered that I could speak some French, deliberately slowed down his speaking pace so that I could better understand him. Obviously sensing my shyness about using my very rusty French, he undertook to help me improve. Already I had been rebuffed by some Parisians who preferred to mock my attempts at speaking French – some pretended not to understand me, although I knew my French was not *that* bad.

Patrick, however, delighted in helping me express myself more clearly and confidently in his native tongue. Each evening as we relaxed in the garden, he would enquire about my day. My language began to flow more easily as I relaxed in Patrick's company; he would ask me questions and help me when I got stuck for words. He also had plenty of questions to ask about Australia and we often talked for an hour or more. I spoke also about my upcoming trip to Romania and flowing on from that he asked me some

From the Ends of the Earth

questions about God. I shudder to think of how my grammar must have sounded at times, but I didn't feel at all self-conscious, just eager to learn and pleased that I was finally able to put my French study to good use.

God had a very good reason for supplying me with a personal French tutor that week, as He was going to use my ability to speak French in Romania very soon afterwards.

Although my oral French needed some practice, my reading skills were serving me well; I relished being able to understand signs, instructions, and inscriptions on plaques. A visit to the Catacombs was particularly moving both for the history, and because I was able to read the French inscriptions of Scripture and poetry engraved on the gravestones within. The reading practice improved my language skills further as my memory was jolted by particular words and phrases which I could in turn put into conversation.

The second reason I was staying in that hostel was an eighteen year old girl named Esther.

I returned to the hostel one evening to discover two new roommates. Four teenagers from England were on their first trip 'abroad' and two of the girls were in my room. Esther settled into the top bunk above my bed, and I was drawn to her, probably because she reminded me a lot of myself at that age - quite shy, a worrier, a bit less sophisticated than the others.

Kathryn Kerridge

One morning when I woke up I noticed a small red Gideon Bible on the floor, almost under my bed. I hadn't noticed it before and asked Esther if it was hers. She said that it was and when I told her that I was a Christian and had my Bible with me, too, her face lit up.

At the time, we were alone in the room and a great conversation about our faith ensued. Esther had just left school and was unsure about her future, although she had a long-held desire to be a nurse and possibly to work in Africa with a Christian organisation. She had been very nervous about her first trip abroad although she was with friends, especially as she didn't speak any French. Her fervent prayer was that there would be an English-speaker in her hostel room and she described her relief when they entered their room and there I was….and a Christian into the bargain! I had prayed before leaving Australia that God would put me in the right place at the right time to be in contact with the right people this whole trip, and here was an example of that answered prayer. Hoping to be an encouragement to her, I gave some examples of God's guidance in my life when I, too, was uncertain about my future.

It's tempting to look now at my photos of these weeks and think that I whipped through it all with great ease. However, my travel journal reveals some great struggles with my health.

From the Ends of the Earth

Interspersed with observations on history, buildings, food, atmosphere and my sense of achievement in negotiating all these new places, modes of transport and getting myself 'unlost', are little panic moments about the state of my body as my energy was quickly ebbing away. No wonder! The previous fortnight had put my body through more intense activity and the least rest I had had since my trip to the USA in 1994.

The enjoyment of my travels was frequently marred by sheer physical fatigue, muscle pain and nausea – and it was difficult not to feel discouraged and a bit numb at times to what I was experiencing, like I was seeing it all through a bit of a fog. Less than a week after arriving in London, I wrote: 'What was I thinking…travelling overseas with ME? …I don't need to pay thousands of dollars to collapse in Europe – I can do that at home!' (As you can tell, on very bad days I completely lost all sense of perspective.) Sometimes tears were close just because I was so bone-weary, and of course every time I faced a challenge or something small went awry, my ability to cope and think on the spot was reduced. Every now and then I fretted about coping with two weeks in Romania, much less the time after that, including an SU camp in Scotland.

As many times as I journalled such thoughts, I was reminded of my calling to Romania and the amount of prayer that had gone into all travel plans I had made, not to mention the faithfulness of God in sustaining me thus far, which in itself was a miracle. The conscious decision *not* to worry or fret my energy away had to be made daily. God had not brought me here to collapse but to fulfil His purposes and to bless me with some of the backpacking travels that I had so longed to be able to do in my twenties. He had not left me 'on the shelf' as I so often felt when I watched my brother and my friends fill this decade of their life with adventures and careers; He had merely waited to bring His plan for me to fulfilment at a different time for a different purpose.

It was brilliant to be adventuring through Europe and learning so much as I navigated my way around on my own, relying on God for even the smallest details, and meeting people of different nationalities. However, travelling solo was also a lonely experience, and I often wished I could share the adventures with a good friend. Andrew was unable to take any further time off work and he was working such long and late shifts (with a lengthy commute) that I barely saw him at night either.

Aloneness had been par for the course in my life over the past decade. Chronic illness makes life lonely in a number of ways – coping daily with a condition that few people understood and which you can't really explain anyway, forced rest at home, working only part-time and having a limited social life. However, this trip was a once-in-a-lifetime experience (so I thought), and it seemed a shame to not be able to share my pleasure and impressions.

This further lesson in God-dependence would serve me in good stead later. This 'once-in-a-lifetime' experience was actually only the beginning of years of ministry travels which would take me all over the world on my own and through many challenging situations far away from family and friends. Without close reliance upon God alone, I would have crumbled under some future pressures I would face. Therefore even this loneliness was part of His plan of equipping.

Solo travel brought more awareness of my interactions with others as for conversation I was forced to chat with people I probably wouldn't even had spoken with had I been with a friend or friends of my own. I doubt I would have received all my French lessons from Patrick, or had such a wonderful talk with Esther had I not been travelling by myself - how much I would have missed had that been the case.

A couple of weeks of sightseeing were great, but there was a restlessness and impatience within me. Much as I had appreciated all the opportunities I had been given to see two of the most amazing and celebrated cities in the world, I was growing dissatisfied with seeing only buildings and monuments. I was itching to get real and personal and share something of God's love with people. I decided that although travel was still on the agenda for the rest of my accrued leave from the library, I wanted to use it for ministry with children. For now, I had

Romania to look forward to, and tired as I was physically, my whole spirit revived at the thought.

From the Ends of the Earth

Chapter 11

Back in London, I settled into a youth hostel in Holland Park and made contact with the South African girl on our Romanian team. We had introduced ourselves via email before I left Australia and planned to meet up in London prior to our Romanian trip.

On a beautifully sunny day we met on Hampstead Heath and talked effortlessly for a couple of hours despite this being our first meeting. The similarities in our faith journeys were striking – of similar age, we both attended Presbyterian churches and had been involved extensively with Scripture Union camping ministries in our respective countries. It 'so happened' that we were booked on the same flight to Romania the following day, even though we had planned our trips from different parts of the world independently of each other.

My backpack weighed a ton, but much of that was composed of various gifts and resources for the Romanian children, so while I staggered around with it for now, at least I knew it wouldn't all be coming back with me! I was stopped at the tube station by an American who 'awarded' me the honour of having the biggest backpack he'd seen on someone my size – it turned out he was a writer for Rough Guide travel books and was on his way to an exotic location armed only with a school-size backpack containing a change of clothes and his toiletries. Oh well, I was still getting used to the whole backpacking thing – travelling light would be a future lesson to learn.

On arrival in Bucharest, we were welcomed by the two other girls in our group (both Americans), a Romanian pastor and his wife, and a Mission Without Borders staff worker. The latter was a girl in her twenties named Cristina, who would act as one of our translators. As I purchased my visa, I soberly reflected on the fact that only ten years previously, when Romania was still under communist rule, there was no way I'd have been allowed into this country as a guest of a Christian organisation. As a child, I knew about Romania as the place where Pastor Richard Wurmbrand spent much of his life imprisoned, undergoing horrendous torture because of his faith. Now I was in that same country openly representing that same faith in God. What a privilege to grow up in Australia where freedom of religion was part of life.

Out of the airport at last, my anticipation grew as the first stop on our itinerary would be the summer camp at which my sponsored child, Florentina, was spending a week. Together with her would be a number of campers also from her children's home. I had come prepared with a colourful backpack as a gift for her, every zip and pocket of which I had filled with small presents. A steady stream of thoughts buzzed through my head as we drew nearer the

From the Ends of the Earth

campsite – would I recognise her from her photo?; How would she respond to me? Would we be able to communicate despite the language barrier?...

The moment our van stopped at the campsite, about 120 curious children descended upon us and we were swept along in the tide of bodies to the dining room where Florentina was. My heart ached to see this tiny little waif of twelve (who was about the size of a healthy Australian seven or eight year old) with spiky blond hair, cut short for hygiene and convenience.

Sitting side-by-side on a little bench under a tree, I presented Florrie with her gifts. Quite shy, she didn't speak much, even though we had a translator nearby, but the look of wonder on her face as she went through that backpack of toys was priceless and no words were needed to convey her thoughts. With each new discovery wide brown eyes, a big smile and a look of amazement clearly said, 'What? Another one? And all for me?' I sat close beside her and hugged her a lot. I was at least able to say the Romanian words for 'I love you'. Imagine being a child abandoned by her parents; imagine almost never hearing those words spoken by people who thought she was precious. I couldn't, not when I had heard that phrase nearly every day of my life even into adulthood, often more than once, and by a number of different people. Growing up, I was in never in doubt of my value to my parents, and yet here I was in the midst of maybe a hundred children who had no concept of what that felt like. How could I begin to comprehend?

Puzzling to me was the number of other children gathered around us who wanted to hug me or hold my hand. One older girl in her late teens especially asked for an introduction as she desired the opportunity to say 'hello' and 'thank you' on behalf of herself and other children. Of course I agreed, but how baffling – after all, I wasn't sponsoring them, neither had I brought gifts for any child apart from Florentina.

Later the reason for their gratitude dawned. Mission Without Borders' strategy was to calculate how many of the total number of children in a home would need sponsors in order to bring in enough income to provide adequate food, clothing, medication and education for *all* the children in that home. Therefore, my sponsorship money for Florentina benefited all the children living with her; they obviously knew this and wanted to thank me for helping them. I was incredibly humbled by this heartfelt show of gratitude – I can't even honestly say that this giving was terribly sacrificial on my part, and yet what a difference it had made to the lives of these young people.

Florentina hoisted her new backpack proudly onto her thin little shoulders and kept a firm grasp of my hand for the next couple of hours – even through dinner, which I had to eat one-handed. Florrie sat on my lap during the Christian Input time which followed the meal, regularly looking up at me with her big brown eyes, almost as if she couldn't believe I was there especially to visit her. We didn't speak much, but I held her close and prayed that she would sense that I cared for her very much. The children sang some of their favourite camp songs, and if we English-speakers recognised the tunes we joined the singing in our language. The Romanian children were delighted that we could all be singing the same songs in two different languages at the same time – especially whenever we got to the word 'Alleluia', which is the same in every language.

Of course, our departure was inevitable, and we eventually walked slowly back towards the van. The moment Florentina realised I was leaving, her face crumpled and she broke into heart-wrenching sobs, her grip on me fiercely tight. Cristina talked soothingly to her, but warned us to make our goodbye short lest Florrie became hysterical. As we drove away, I was very shaken – haunted by the image of this pathetic little figure standing in the doorway in her grubby camp clothes, tears streaming down her face, clutching a pad of paper and some crayons from the little backpack she still wore on her shoulders. I felt so heartless and cruel leaving her behind.

I wouldn't have missed that visit for the world, but I had to wonder whether the effect of it on Florentina would be more negative than positive. Here was a child who had been abandoned by the adults who

Kathryn Kerridge

should have treasured her most – was I just another who had walked in and out of her life in a few hours? Would she not feel abandoned yet again? Cristina, experienced as she was with sponsor visits, obviously read my thoughts. She reassured me that Florentina would now know that someone loved her so much that they came from the other side of the world just to see her, and every time I wrote to her she would remember that.

The summer camp at which we volunteers would spend a week was in a gorgeous country location in the Lotrioara Valley. Although our camp information had stated that facilities would be basic and that we would be bathing in the stream (at home I had my hair cut short so it would be less fuss) and using port-a-loos, a surprise awaited us. Just two weeks prior to our arrival, construction had been completed on two flushing toilets and two hot-water showers for us to use. What an honour!

The children would be sleeping in bright yellow tents (a novelty for them), but for us there were two twin bedrooms above the kitchen building. What provision this turned out to be – not only did this result in more restful sleep, but also a measure of privacy and a haven in which to shelter for brief moments during the week from the intensity of the camp experience. We had no idea how emotionally draining the week would be, but God obviously did and provided for us accordingly. Our translation team for the week consisted of Cristina, along with an eighteen year old

From the Ends of the Earth

girl (Anca) from a local church, and to some extent, Alex, the MWB Romania director's ten year old son.

Although I had attended more Christian camps in my life than I could count, summer camp in Romania was quite a different kettle of fish. In many respects, children are the same all around the world...they love to laugh, play games, sing and eat, but there were quite a few adjustments to be made being at camp with children from the homes.

I found it difficult to deal with the pushing and shoving. The young people had little concept of standing in a line, or waiting patiently for a turn at anything, whether it be for craft kits or sweets or balloon animals or face-painting. The jostling was quite fierce as we were confronted with a sea of grabbing hands waving in our faces. My natural inclination was to be rather like a school teacher who would send a 'grabbing' child to the end of the line (except there was never such a line in existence).

I had to realise that such behaviour was fuelled by a fear of missing out. I came from a culture of abundance - whether you were served first or last there was generally still enough food, toys, attention, whatever, to go around. These children had no such assurance. When treats were offered, the fear was if they didn't get in first, they would miss out. Little faces would fall when we packed up our activities at the end of free time, and children weren't always convinced when we tried to assure them that there was more for the next day and everyone would get a turn.

Furthermore, the children had grown up not with parents or families who taught them basic manners or etiquette, but in children's homes where life could be quite rough. Although in many homes the staff were loving and caring, trying to do the best they could with what they had, time and resources were in too short a supply to properly parent or to be able to stamp out the inevitable instances of bullying. I could hardly be angry at children who didn't know any better – after all, I had loving parents and teachers who taught me these things, and I hadn't been abandoned and left to my own devices to survive. Still, I found the noise and lack of order wearing at times.

Mealtimes were another learning experience. The food was calorie-heavy and plentiful, and the average camper could put on up to five pounds in weight over the course of just one week – not due to overeating but simply because they were having enough to eat for once. Many of the campers' bodies were clearly malnourished and thin, and they tucked heartily into the food, often demolishing second and third helpings. In fact, there was so much food at the first meal of camp that the children had a hard time believing it wasn't a one-off treat, but that there would be food like this three times *every* day *all* week, with snacks in between.

It was not unusual to find that on the first day some children had hidden extra bread in their pockets just in case there wasn't any or enough the next day. Experience in the orphanages had taught that just because there was food one day was no guarantee there would be any the next.

One eighteen year old girl told me that for her, the best thing about summer camp was that it was the only week in the whole year that she wasn't hungry every day. You would never even *think* of having a food fight at a camp like this; food was just too precious a commodity to be wasted.

For quite a while after I arrived back in Australia, I found that I couldn't watch or participate in games involving food without thinking of those Romanian children and feeling sick that we could just throw it around. I still find it hard to see food thrown away, even though I know that to some extent this is unavoidable for health and safety reasons. The feeling of discomfort serves to remind me that I have no just cause to complain about food in any way – ever!

The lack of structure at camp was another adjustment. Meals and small group Bible teaching sessions had set times, but the rest of the day flowed more or less as the children wished. The purpose was to provide a real holiday as far removed as possible from the structured life of the institutions in which they lived. Very little freedom of choice was part of life in the children's homes, but at camp choice abounded - what games to play and when, when to go to bed, and even whether or not to bathe each day (although swims in the river were strongly encouraged!). We rarely went to bed before 12.30-1.00am, as many of the teenagers wanted to sing, talk and play music late into the night to prolong their precious camp days as much as possible.

Although we understood why this was so, combining lack of sleep and the emotional impact of discovering more about the deprived lives of the campers resulted in shattering fatigue for us. I may have been exhausted, but I was still standing (most of the time). Considering the toll that the week was clearly taking on the other three – all fairly fit and robust - the fact that I was keeping up with them was a miracle...once again, God at work; faithful in enabling me to do what He called me to do.

The week remains in my mind as a kaleidoscope of ever-changing emotions – joy and laughter, heartbreaking sadness, peace, love, discomfort, weariness, frustration, the works. Camp was a blur of experiences – physically trying to keep up the pace in a tired body, mentally coping with the language barrier, and emotionally dealing with the heartrending life stories of people so young, all took a toll. It was impossible to fully process all the experiences at the time - in fact I ceased to have the energy and the words to write in my travel journal during this week of camp, other than make a list of what we did and little incidents that touched my heart. Camp became a series of snapshots of events that opened my eyes to the plight of the thousands of abandoned young people of Romania in stark contrast to the privilege, love and comparative wealth that characterised my own upbringing.

Many times the sheer enormity of the issues of rejection, abandonment and poverty that these young people faced was overwhelming. As I had felt during that short visit to Florentina, I couldn't help wondering if what we were doing for such a short time would really do any good in the overall scheme of their lives. However, there were many little incidents during the week which reassured me that even small things done with the love of God could make an indelible imprint.

On the second day of camp out we produced string and beads for bracelet-making. The children were still adjusting to our presence and communication was very limited, which we found quite frustrating. The whole craft exercise took less than an hour, and yet one of the Christian volunteers at the camp approached at the end to tell us not to worry about the language barrier. 'They already know you love them,' she said.

Puzzled, we asked her how they could know this. 'Because you knelt down on the ground to help them,' was the reply. We struggled to understand how such an act could signify anything special. I couldn't see how I could have helped any of the children *without* getting down to their level and being close to them.

My heart ached inside when it was explained that very few adults would bother to do such a thing for these children. However, if something so simple could express love to them, we girls were determined to make sure that all of these campers would go home at the end of the week having no doubt that someone loved and cared for them, and that God loved and cared for them. Clearly we didn't need fluent Romanian language to do that; our actions would speak very loudly.

So for the next week we brushed hair (even hair that wasn't very clean), gave hugs, held hands, painted faces, sat beside and paid lots of attention to these precious children. It didn't take long for the younger ones to feel comfortable with us as we showed our love in these simple practical ways. Some of the older teenagers took a little longer to trust us but a surprising breakthrough came one day thanks so a sack of potatoes.

A couple of days into camp, Cristina approached us with the suggestion that we spend a day serving the cooks, helping them with their huge job of preparing meals for all these hungry mouths. We agreed without hesitation. For our first task, we were led to a big sack full of potatoes, some knives and a couple

From the Ends of the Earth

of big cooking pots. We set to work peeling the spuds for dinner.

Even with the four of us plus Cristina and Anca, the job was tedious and lengthy and made even more difficult by the fact that our tools were small and not very sharp. Before long, our peeling fingers were red and rubbed and our backs were aching, but we kept our spirits up by singing all the praise songs we could think of.

Halfway through the seemingly bottomless sack, as we sang and talked, we became aware of curious eyes intently watching from the sides of the meal tent, many of which belonged to these uncommunicative teenagers. We kept on with our task, feeling the stares boring into our backs, but each of us silently praying for a way to get through to these young people who seemed so unwilling to accept us.

Finally, the bottom of the sack was visible and we triumphantly carted the pots of potatoes to the cooks. After a welcome break and then lunch, we reported to the cooks for our next instructions.

Our hearts sank when we were pointed towards another huge sack of potatoes. My blistered fingers on my right hand made me wish that I was ambidextrous. Still, there was nothing to be done but to take up our little knives again and remember that we had come here to serve God no matter what we were asked to do. Sore fingers and a little bit of pain and discomfort was a small price to pay to help give these children full stomachs.

No sooner had we picked up our first potatoes from the sack when we were joined one after the other by six or eight teenagers…the ones who had been watching so intently before lunch. They filtered in, picked up a knife and sat on the benches with us, and before too long were chatting away to us with Cristina and Anca translating.

The sudden change in attitude toward us was bewildering but Cristina brought enlightenment later on. At first these hardened teenagers looked upon us suspiciously as 'do-gooders', wondering why we would come all the way from our 'rich' countries to be at camp with them – did we just want to be nosy about their difficult lives, or did we perhaps want something from them or just make ourselves look good? When they saw us peeling that first sack of potatoes with smiles and songs, they realised that we were truly here to serve them and not for our own gain, and that broke the barriers down.

That second sack of potatoes was peeled in half the time by twice as many hands, and with much laughter, singing and serious questions about God. We had earned the right to speak about our faith and our lives, all because of a sack of humble potatoes and a few old knives.

From the Ends of the Earth

It was also about this time that I understood why God had arranged my impromptu French lessons with Patrick the previous week at the youth hostel in Paris.

Several of the older Romanian girls and boys who couldn't speak any English learned French at school, and when they discovered I could speak a little of the language as well were delighted that we had a way of communicating apart from translation. I was aware of some of them watching me during the week, and wondered what was going through their minds. Were they suspicious of me?...did they like me?...did they even want to talk to me?...It turned out that they actually *had* wanted to chat but weren't confident enough to do so through the translation process with crowds of other campers watching, and they felt overshadowed by those campers who could speak some English.

Now that we had a common language, I was able to have many direct conversations with these teenagers during the week, and they in turn were clearly pleased that they had a special way of communicating with me.

Sometimes it's a long time before it becomes plain how God will use some of the experiences of our lives, but He wastes nothing. If I spent seven and a half years studying French at high school and university, and a week in that Paris hostel to brush it up just for this week in Romania, it was worth it!

Kathryn Kerridge

Camp was full of special occasions and treats for the campers aside from abundant food.

One was an excursion to the Sibiu public pool. As one of the American girls and I dived in to race some of the boys who challenged us, we were aware of some approving glances and comments – and somehow we knew it wasn't because of how we looked in our swimsuits! Through translation, we discovered that the admiration was for our diving and swimming ability. I hadn't thought twice about this, as I had (along with most Australian children) learnt to swim at a very young age; fun in the water (via the beach and backyard pools) was a way of life for us. Of course most of these Romanian children didn't have anyone to teach them how to swim, let alone take them to the pool for an afternoon of fun as my mum had often done for Andrew and me and our friends.

As we splashed happily away in the warm water, onto our heads rained a sudden bombardment of shampoo sachets. A cunning strategy to ensure that campers get a proper cleaning at least once during the week is a trip to the pool and its showers. It works in Australia; it works in Romania too!

Several young people collected up some sachets and hurried immediately to the showers at the side of the pool to use their precious shampoo straight away. Five minutes, then ten minutes went by, and they were still standing blissfully under the showers, two or three bodies apiece. I couldn't understand why they would want to get out of the pool early just to have a shower. Swimming was a treat they could rarely enjoy while living at the orphanage, so why not make the most of it?

It turned out that having a hot shower every day was also a luxury that orphanage life didn't afford. Not only was hot or warm water with which to bathe unlikely, daily bathing often wasn't possible, and even soap not always available.

No wonder children continued to stand under these warm showers, shampooing their hair again and again, and washing their whole bodies with the silky smooth liquid. Many never entered the pool again that day, such was their rapture. As I went to have my own shower, I was met with broad smiles and was urged to hurry up and try it and see how wonderful it felt! How incomprehensible to them to know that I could do this every day as many times as I wanted.

I stood under the shower trying to imagine what they were experiencing, slathering my whole head and body in as much foamy shampoo as I wanted for as long as I wanted, *really* concentrating on the smooth and silky sensation of the fragrant liquid on my skin. Truly it did feel luxurious and extravagant, and I'm sure the enraptured smile on my face matched those of the campers.

Kathryn Kerridge

On the last day of camp, everyone was gathered together in the meal tent for a presentation ceremony. Each young person was given a certificate congratulating them on an individual accomplishment, together with a cuddly toy. To be given a toy each for their very own brought broad smiles to faces and even the eighteen and nineteen year old boys held them close. Many of the children had never or had only rarely been given a gift at all in their lives, let alone one in conjunction with being recognised for an achievement. There was therefore no shame in clutching a cuddly toy tightly no matter what age one was.

After all the campers' names had been called out, we girls were surprised and delighted to hear our names being called out as well. We, too, received a camp certificate and cuddly toy, in my case a lovely jointed teddy bear. Miki, one of the older boys with whom I had been speaking in French during the week, immediately grabbed a ballpoint pen and wrote his name and 'Je t'aime' ('I love you') on the bear's paws, with the injunction, 'Don't forget me.'

Miki wasn't the only camper to express that sentiment; these young people knew that we volunteers would be leaving after camp, but they had such an obvious desire to be remembered, to be considered still important, long after we physically departed. We were farewelled with much affection, and I was incredibly moved and humbled by two very special gifts.

From the Ends of the Earth

One teenage girl, Dani, had attached herself to me during the week of camp, and was almost always by my side holding my hand or with her arm around my waist. She was obviously starved for love and affection – she never received any visits from her family at the orphanage and at nineteen was on her own in the world. We had managed to communicate quite well even with her limited English and my very limited Romanian, and she had even begun doing a little translating between me and other children.

The day before we were to leave camp, a group of us, including Dani, went for a walk to the river, and she mentioned something about having a surprise for me. A little later in the afternoon, as I was packing my backpack, she came to ask for a plastic bag. I absently handed her the only one I had, a fairly small one, and she replied it wasn't really big enough, but it would do. Soon she returned to me with that bag, crammed with something wrapped in plain white butcher paper. It was handed to me with the words, 'This is for you because I think you will like it.' However, her firm instructions were not to open it until after I left camp, so I hugged her and thanked her and packed the gift in my luggage.

That night it was difficult to get Dani to go to bed – she knew that the following day was the last time we would ever see each other. A few of us stayed up chatting and praying in the now quiet campsite, and Dani became more emotional. I was praying and racking my brain to think of something I could say to her that would have some lasting impact – into my mind came the idea of us being *sisters* in Christ and therefore *family* – words that were meaningful to Dani in her situation. I handed her the brightly coloured Mickey Mouse cap that I had been wearing during the week, and wrote a little message on the inside. She immediately put it on and kept it there. I wondered if she was going to sleep in it as well! I sent her off to bed before she became too distressed, and settled down in my own bed to try to get some sleep.

As I did so, the package Dani had given me that afternoon caught my eye, and I confess that, overpowered by my curiosity, I opened it. Wrapped in the torn triangle of white paper was the cuddly racoon she had received with her camp diploma that afternoon. Dani had just given me one of the few presents that she had ever received in her life. My first thought was that I couldn't keep something that was so precious to her and that I would have to give it back! Of course, that was impossible without her knowing it had been opened contrary to her instructions... then I realised that its value to her was exactly the reason I *had* to keep it. What a humbling lesson in sacrificial giving from someone who had very little materially to give, and it made me ashamed at my own selfish tendencies.

Camp was over and we were driven back to the MWB apartment in Sibiu by Marius, the camp director. Florin, one of the teenage kitchen helpers,

From the Ends of the Earth

had come along for the ride and he helped to carry our luggage up the stairs. Florin had barely spoken a word to me all week, but was constantly smiling and making sure I had enough food. During the bus ride to the pool, when I had leant my head against the window to try to have a little nap, he had told off one of the other girls for trying to talk to me – 'Ssshh, she's sleeping!' was the translation I heard later. Florin was like a guardian angel, and his constant care and concern for me and my health touched me deeply.

At the top of the stairs, he turned to say goodbye and give me his wide gap-toothed smile one last time, and as he did so he thrust his new little purple bear from the camp presentation into my hands. He pointed to where he'd written his name on the tag around the bear's neck, so I would remember him. I had barely spoken a few words to him all week, and yet he considered me worthy of such a treasured gift. I had thought my trip to Romania would be all about me giving to people, but I felt that I had received so much more in so many ways than I gave.

Mission Without Borders continues to hold summer camps each year in all six field countries.

After camp, it was time to observe some other aspects of the MWB ministry. We spent some time in the main office in Sibiu; explored the warehouse with shelf upon shelf of clothes, toys, blankets, food parcels and medication for distribution to families and homes; and visited two children's homes, one for two to eight year olds, and one for teenage girls. We were even interviewed by a Christian radio station about our trip, and why we would come from so far away as America, South Africa and Australia to show love and care to abandoned Romanian children who are considered the dregs of society in that country.

On the one hand, it was wonderful to see more about the work of MWB close up, but my body, mind and emotions were completely spent by this stage even though I'd only been in the country a week. My smiling façade finally crumbled beneath the load of my sheer physical exhaustion, and one day I just sat on the steps of the office and burst into tears. The other girls gathered around me to pray and with God's renewed strength I made it through the rest of the day, but had to go to bed once back at the apartment while the others went on an evening dinner and shopping excursion to Sibiu.

I was grateful to be in bed so early and with some quiet time on my own, but struggled with disappointment at missing out on the rest of the evening's plans, especially seeing Revolution Square, scene of two days of fighting during the 1989 revolution. Sometimes I found it so difficult to understand why God didn't heal me. All I wanted to do was serve Him with my life; surely I would be of more use to Him healthy that with this darned ME that limited me in so many ways.

Still, I knew I was actually living a miracle - I might still have ME, but I had gone from working part-time in a library to being here in Romania, almost four weeks into an intense overseas trip, and I was still functioning. Struggling, yes, but not collapsed and bedridden, as really should have been the case after pushing my body so hard. Rather than focus on the one thing I was forced to miss, I had to choose to see what God had enabled me to do. I had a great deal to be thankful for, but I still had to conscientiously cultivate an attitude of gratitude when I didn't *feel* like praising God.

God continued His faithfulness to me and that trip to Sibiu was the only thing I missed during my time in Romania (apart from some of the scenery during our long drives, when my eyes couldn't stay open and I slept). We spent the next four days sightseeing the country's natural and architectural beauty and history as we slowly made our way back to Bucharest.

Our absorption in the plight of abandoned children and the work of MWB made it difficult to adjust to the 'rich' tourist role, especially when I personally knew so many young people that would be going to bed hungry each night. Still, I knew it was a necessary reconciliation with my own culture that must be made in order for this mission trip to be an overall positive experience rather than a soul-destroying one. The 'reverse culture-shock' kicked in, and would continue during my remaining time in Europe before I returned to my home in Australia. God would use my next little 'mission', an SU camp in Scotland, to continue this adjustment.

Back in London I had a few days to chill out and do my laundry before boarding a train to Edinburgh. The noise, size and wealth of London was a huge shock to my system, but at the same time there was something comforting about returning to 'my' reality after the emotional turmoil of the previous fortnight. I remember feeling disappointed when first told that the trip to Romania would be only two weeks long (I had been hoping for a month), but God clearly knew what I would be able to cope with – and this time, two weeks was it.

One thing I decided to do in London was finally replace my huge backpack with one that was more my size. Andrew wanted one for his travels and mine was the right size for his six-foot three-inch frame. I bought a green and black one that was quite a lot smaller, but just right for me to carry. I was finally learning the lesson of travelling light.

From the Ends of the Earth

Chapter 12

On July 27 it was time to head for Scotland, so I journeyed four and a half hours north by train to Edinburgh. I was pretty weary so unfortunately couldn't keep my eyes open to enjoy the scenery. I did, however, manage to be awake when the train crossed the English/Scottish border. My first impression of the country was that the grass was such a lush shade of green it was almost fluorescent...well, compared with the sage green colours of the Australian landscape anyway. This was obviously a benefit of the infamous abundance of Scottish rain.

Once again I was in tourist mode, this time among sights such as Edinburgh Castle, the Palace of Holyroodhouse, John Knox's House and St Giles' Cathedral. Strolling along the Royal Mile, I never tired of cobbled streets, ancient buildings and the all-pervading presence of the Castle on the hill, high above the city. Another living history lesson and I loved it all.

The Museum of Childhood had a particular impact – familiar toys of the 70s and 80s brought to mind birthdays and Christmases gone by when I received many of them as presents.

Wandering through the museum for a couple of hours, I was overwhelmed with gratitude for my childhood – for parents who loved and cared enough to give me gifts; for life in a family with the financial resources to supply many treats in addition to the bare necessities; for the simple fact of growing up in a secure family unit. My childhood was so blessed, happy and secure in comparison with that of the young people I met in Romania and I was ashamed for the times I had taken it all for granted or had been ungrateful.

Almost a decade later, I remain eternally thankful for the changes wrought in me during these travels which took me out of the comfort zone of my comfortable life. I am a far more grateful person for everything from material blessings to a loving family to my religious freedom. I still hate to see food thrown away, and I find it hard to complain about paying tax, when it means I have a job and the benefit of health care, education and decent roads. It's amazing what a difference two weeks can make!

At the time, though, the process of adjustment continued. The next phase was camp at Lendrick Muir, SU Scotland's residential activity centre in Perthshire. This was not your average 'campsite' but a massive 150-bed Georgian-style country house dating back to the mid-1800s. I was staggered. This was camping the 'posh' way – warm duvets on the beds, central heating, Italian plaster ceilings, and even some stained glass windows. Oh, my!

From the Ends of the Earth

For the next seven days and nights, my group of primary school-aged girls and I did all the normal 'camp' stuff; much the same as an SU camp back home in Queensland, except I was wearing many more clothes. This was summer, but I was freezing. Brisbane in *winter* didn't get this cold! I was the subject of much hilarity, bundled up when the children were wearing shorts and singlet tops. I didn't care what anyone said - eighteen degrees Celsius was *not* 'roasting'!

Camp was second nature to me, but this one was difficult in several respects. Firstly, I was physically stretched to my limit. Thankfully God had provided a very compassionate team leader, and I was able to have some breaks during which I slept like a log in the leaders' room for a precious hour or two. As for the rest of the time, the sheer empowering of God carried me through – there is no other explanation.

As difficult as the exhaustion was, I had as much difficulty adjusting to some behaviour and attitudes of these predominantly middle-class campers which clashed violently with my recent experience in Romania.

At mealtimes, some children turned up their noses at dinners which they didn't like, or left mounds of unwanted food on their plates. I struggled to bite my tongue when internally I was fuming, 'Don't you know there are kids your age in Romania who are going to bed hungry and only get enough to eat when they are at camp? STOP COMPLAINING!'

Of course it would have been entirely inappropriate and unfair to try to impose my recent and still raw experience on eleven year olds who had not seen or heard what I had. I gritted my teeth and remembered that this was the reality of living in a world of plenty where children saw it as their right to have just what they wanted, and lots of it. The truth was that this was often my attitude too, and I could not become all pious following a smidgeon of mission work amidst poverty. Camp in Scotland was as much about God helping me re-settle into my own culture as it was about sharing the good news of Jesus with the young people. Despite my personal struggles, I had a fabulous week of activity with the campers and team.

It was an amazing experience to work with Scripture Union volunteers in Scotland who were on the same mission as SU volunteers in Queensland. I didn't properly meet any SU Scotland staff but hoped to stay in touch with a few of my campers and fellow team members. Departing Scotland, I was very thankful for the week of ministry and the opportunity to visit this pretty country.

After another week in London, a weekend in Belgium with my brother and his friend was an opportunity for one last use of my French before flying home to Brisbane. By the time I arrived home, my Romanian experiences had been sufficiently processed so that when people greeted me with, 'So, how was Romania?' I could honestly say – 'Hard, but good', without feeling that the burden of what I had experienced was eating me up inside.

There ended another two months of travel and ministry, another two months of seeing God's miraculous provision and care not only in the physical sense but in so many other ways. As I was forced to rely upon His strength and guidance in new and intense circumstances, He proved Himself faithful every time.

Kathryn Kerridge

Chapter 13

Clearly, over the years God's 'School of Life' had taught me many valuable lessons.

Instead of changing my health circumstances (i.e. healing me outright), God had been using *them* to change *me*. He had accomplished a great deal of character refining as He brought natural tendencies into balance and filtered out of me a lot of the rubbish. The rabid perfectionist who beat herself up mercilessly when things didn't work out 100% perfectly had disappeared. I still tended to have high standards, but I also knew when a job was good enough and how to be content with my best according to the health that I had. I had learned how to feel secure in my value to God and not to base my identity on my achievements. I had learned the futility of comparing my life with others and letting that dictate my feelings of success or failure. I had learned a greater level of love and compassion for others through suffering, and had developed a great deal of patience with myself and my 'slow' body as well as with others. I had learned to be flexible and much more laid back about life.

I had come to know and understand God in ways I never would have done otherwise. I learned to 'expect the unexpected' answers to prayer, and not to get so focused on my own expectations and plans

From the Ends of the Earth

that I missed what God was actually doing. I realised that God is often accused of not answering prayers, when in reality His answers are sometimes unnoticed because they come when and where we least expect. It is then we tend towards disillusionment and disappointment and of course, omit to thank Him. God was teaching me more and more to see things from His point of view; to 'have the mind of Christ', and to let go of my own agenda.

The brutal truth is that the world does not revolve around *me*. As a follower of Christ, my life is not about attaining my own comfort and goals or primarily serving *my* needs, but about reaching out to others in service as an example of practical Christianity. If continuing to live with ME was God's way of having me do that, then okay. However, my world also does not revolve around ME. Chronic illness need not define nor confine me. My value and identity is in Christ, and He is able to accomplish whatever He desires through me regardless of the state of my physical health.

Instead of healing me in order to fulfil His purposes in my latest adventure, God had sustained me in ways I cannot explain. This was evident not only to me, but to many others. A couple of days after my arrival home, I returned to work. A colleague who spied me as I signed in exclaimed, 'What are you doing here?' before she even said 'Hello' or 'Welcome home'! A bit taken aback, and uncertain as to her meaning, I replied that I was rostered on to work that day. 'I know,' she said, 'but we were expecting you to have to take at least a week off on sick leave because of your health! How are you still standing after that trip?'

There really was only one answer I could possibly give – 'God!' Whether others believed in Him or not, I was living testimony to something out of the ordinary going on. Staff who saw me year after year working only part-time and who knew that on a 'bad' day I struggled through each hour, now saw me able to work after eight weeks of travel and mission. Yes, I was pretty tired (to say the least), and it took months of extra rest and semi-hibernation for my body to recover, but I did not have to take any sick leave and was able to fulfil my responsibilities, and that was a miracle.

God also used my testimony of His strength in my weakness as an encouragement to other Christians. Christian friends and a supportive church family had faithfully prayed for and supported me during my trip, and it was wonderful to stand before them one Sunday and tell of my experiences and how their prayers for my health and safety were answered. That, in turn, encouraged their own faith and inspired their prayer lives.

The life of one of my oldest friends was impacted in a way I never expected. Our friendship dated back to primary school, and while she had become a Christian at an SU camp in high school, she had drifted from her faith in her twenties. Our lives had diverged for a number of years, but we were once again regularly in touch. During a visit to her after I returned from Romania, one of her first questions was, 'How did you cope with the food?'

For three years prior to my trip, I had followed a strict gluten-free diet, discovering through trial and error that eating gluten (the protein found in wheat, oats, barley and rye) exacerbated my fatigue and other symptoms of ME. It was a bit of a nuisance to follow – cutting out staple foods such as bread, pasta and most cereals meant a lot more advance planning, not to mention that I had always loved my carbs. In addition, lots of other products such as canned soups and baked beans that contained wheat as a thickener had to go, but within weeks there was enough of a positive difference in my health to stick with it despite the inconvenience, and it soon became a way of life that didn't bother me at all. I just took along a bag of my own foods to camps, and the cooks didn't mind if I went in and out of the kitchen as I needed. If I went out to dinner, the restaurant could be phoned in advance for menu choices.

One of the challenges of travelling was how to maintain that diet to keep my health stable as I was backpacking and doing mission work in a country where I could not be too fussy due to the limited availability of foods, and because I did not want to culturally offend by refusing what was served to me. I had ordered gluten-free meals for the plane but within a few days of arrival in England realised the difficulty of eating gluten-free for two months.

The availability of gluten-free foods in supermarkets at the time was much more limited than at home, and what was available in health food shops was prohibitively expensive. Furthermore, most youth hostels included breakfast in their prices, and as I was paying about fifty Australian dollars per night just for a dorm bed, I couldn't afford *not* to eat a full free breakfast – cereal, toast, yoghurt, fruit, eggs, beans and fruit juice. If I ate everything I was entitled to eat at breakfast, I only needed one other meal that day.

The bottom line was that either I would be fasting a lot or else including gluten in my diet for the first time in three years, praying that my body coped without an adverse affect on my symptoms. I have to confess that although I was a bit afraid of the consequences, I was delighted to be able to indulge in bread, bagels and pasta, and I found the fresh Romanian bread we were served in abundance at summer camp irresistible.

As the weeks went by, I could feel my body gradually feeling more 'toxic', but I was able to keep going without suffering any stomach upsets, headaches or excess fatigue from the change in diet. That in itself was amazing. By the time eight weeks passed and I was home again, my body definitely felt overloaded and I was glad enough to go back to my former dictary restrictions, but the point was that God had been true to His promises of supplying me with the strength and physical ability to do the job He had called me to do. Once again, He seemed to have suspended the natural laws of how my body worked for the necessary amount of time – no more; no less.

When my friend had heard that I had to revert to all the foods I would normally avoid and yet suffered almost none of the side effects, she exclaimed, 'Now I know I *have* to start going to church again!'

For the previous year or so, she had come across Christians and other circumstances that had been pointing her back to God, but she had kept trying to postpone the issue and ignore them. Upon hearing my 'gluten' story, she felt she could no longer ignore God's power and the need for her to sort out her relationship with Him. Apparently, this was 'the last straw' for her resistance. Soon after, I experienced the joy of sitting beside one of my oldest friends at church Sunday after Sunday as she began to attend and to bring along her young daughter to 'KidZone'.

Not for the first time did I recall the desperate prayer I had prayed during my year in bed, asking that whatever else happened, God would do something good with the situation so it wasn't a waste. Turns out He would keep answering it for the rest of my life.

Kathryn Kerridge

Chapter 14

Life quickly settled back into its normal routine but there was still the matter of my four weeks' annual leave to use by the end of the financial year. By then I'd have accrued another four weeks for the year I was currently working. How could I best use the time, since I obviously wouldn't be able to accumulate that much leave again in this job? Almost before the question was asked, the sense came that God was opening the door for a return to the USA.

Away for two months, I'd scarcely been home two months, and now I was thinking of going to America in eight months for two months. What?! For years and years it felt like God was hardly moving me along at all, but He was clearly making up for lost time now.

Permission was granted for me to take one month's leave in June 2000 and the other month's leave in July of that year. Straddling two financial years, my employer was satisfied and I had a-two month block of time in which to go back to America.

Hmm....where exactly to go? My previous camp directors, John and Fay, were no longer in a camping ministry. Applying through a camp counsellor agency wasn't an option as I wasn't available for a full summer season. This meant I couldn't get a visa

From the Ends of the Earth

through an agency in order to receive any 'pocket money'. However, I would happily pay my own way to a Christian camp, asking only food and accommodation. Although the camp would only have me for two months, I would be almost a 'free' worker but of course they would have to accept my physical limitations.

A friend of John and Fay was the Director of a Presbyterian camp in Montana and he agreed I could work at his camp for the time I could give. My arrival was scheduled for the start of summer staff training in mid-June.

For the two weeks prior to camp that I would be in the States, I arranged to spend a week in California with the two American girls with whom I went to Romania, and then a week with John and Fay and family, now living in Oregon. It had been six years since I had seen these dear friends, and I couldn't wait! All those years of asking God if I could return to the USA for more camp ministry and He had finally said 'Yes'.

My travel agent ('Where are you going *this* time?!') was on the case finding the best airfare and I began planning and preparing for my next mission journey.

Around this time my work situation had become quite difficult, primarily on a health level. A library assistant job can be very physical (no, we don't sit around reading books all day, contrary to popular belief), involving a fair amount of lifting, bending and reaching. Recurring pain in my shoulders and neck due to the repetitive nature of some of this work was a result and along with a few other staff members, I was seeing a physiotherapist contracted by the Council. Daily muscle and joint pain and achiness plagued me as a result of having ME; I certainly didn't need additional stress on my body.

As the time drew closer for my much-anticipated return to America, I presented God with some good reasons to resign from the library altogether. That would eliminate the 'health hazard' I felt my job had become and allow me to spend the entire summer of camp in Montana, instead of the wrench of leaving two-thirds of the way through. However much I wrestled with this issue, in the end I felt strongly not to make a rash decision out of frustration, but to stay with my job, have my two-month break and reassess things afterwards.

At the beginning of June I was back at Brisbane International Airport with my guitar and backpack ready to fly to LA once again. Soon after I arrived home from my 1994 trip to America, in the window of jeweller's shop I noticed an unusual gold ring in the shape of the skyline of New York City. Immediately I bought it as a symbol which I could wear daily to remind me of God's faithfulness to me on that trip. It also served as a kind of prayer that I could return to the USA one day. Six years later, I sat on a plane wearing that ring and living the answer to that prayer.

In California, I had a wonderful reunion with my two friends from Romania, both of whom worked for Mission Without Borders in LA. Accompanying them at work for a couple of days I was able to see more aspects of the mission's work, meet other staff, and share memories of the previous summer's trip. Furthermore, my two personal tour guides showed me more of California, from Beverly Hills to Santa Barbara.

A week later, I was back at the airport to catch my flight to Oregon. John and Fay's children were children no longer! Zach was now a sixteen year old learning to drive, Rachel was fourteen and about to graduate from Junior High and Joel was twelve and taller than me. Again I was accepted as part of the family, and I was also able to meet up with a couple of other Geneva Hills summer staff girls; one was married and the other engaged - I appreciated meeting their husband and fiancé.

A week after that, I landed at the tiny Kalispell airport. Montana is the fourth largest state of the USA in terms of land measure but has fewer than one million people, making it very sparsely populated. I hadn't known too much about the state before my research in preparation for my trip, other than that it provided the spectacular scenery for films such as 'A River Runs Through It' and 'The Horse Whisperer'.

Kathryn Kerridge

Spectacular scenery indeed – Glacier Camp was situated in the west of the state on the shore of Flathead Lake (the largest body of fresh water west of the Mississippi) and opposite the Mission Mountains. I was stunned into silence by breathtaking views of the lake and mountains which were still snow-capped this early in the summer. It was about as contrasting a view as possible from the golden beaches of sunny Queensland…and the temperature was rather different, too. Montana was stunningly beautiful, but oh, so cold – in fact, it felt like winter to me. (I wasn't the only one – on staff that summer was a guy from Jamaica and his definition of summer was pretty similar to mine.)

During our two weeks of counsellor training, I was the source of much amusement for the other members of the staff, partly because I was so wrapped up in fleeces, gloves, jeans and warm hats; and partly because my accent apparently made me sound so much like Steve Irwin, the Crocodile Hunter, who was hitting the zenith of his fame in the USA. Two of the guys in particular were huge Steve fans, and one day when we were shopping for craft supplies in the local Wal-Mart store, an inflatable crocodile made its way into our purchases. The boys spent the ride back to camp inventing the justification of this expense to the camp director.

The decision was soon vindicated as the croc became an indispensible tool in our morning Bible teaching times. Those two guys managed to incorporate it into sketches and drama almost every day, and the campers absolutely loved it. Bet you never thought that a lesson on the 'armour of God' (Ephesians 6) could be effectively illustrated with the aid of an inflatable crocodile!

Surrounded by the exquisite beauty of God's creation, I would awaken early and have my quiet time with God at one of the outdoor chapels which overlooked the water and the mountains. I was overwhelmed with thankfulness that in His perfect time, He had brought me back to this country and to this incredible place to work with another wonderful group of people.

Once again God's hand of blessing was evident all around, not only in the natural beauty around me. The camp and the programme itself were perfect for an Aussie like me who loved the outdoors. Days were filled with activities such as hiking, outdoor games, a high ropes course and giant swing, a bouldering wall, swimming, canoeing and kayaking in the lake, and getting creative in the well-stocked craft cabin. And in what seemed like a hilarious joke just between God and me – the camp had recently purchased....A Blob! What are the odds of that?!

Here I had been praying for six years to return to the USA for another camp and God had sent me to one of the few with a Blob! Yes, whatever His reasons for delaying my return until now, His timing was perfect, and through this big, giant, stripy pillow of air, He was just reminding me that He sees every desire of my heart and fulfils dreams in His own unique ways, and with a sense of humour.

I had wondered about how I would fit in with the rest of the staff, who would have either just finished high school or be college students while here I was at the grand old age of twenty-nine. That, combined with my need for extra rest, would surely make me look like a bit of a 'granny'. I needn't have worried – they were full of encouragement, support and lots of little gifts as well, when they discovered that I wasn't being paid. I was included in any plans for days off, and no offence was taken if I wasn't well enough to go.

Many enjoyable hours were passed as we wandered around Wal-Mart and the Christian bookstore in Kalispell on days off, and I had my first experience of white-water rafting on the Clark Fork River – yes, it was a fairly gentle flow, but adventurous enough for my first time...Not to mention a chance to don the wetsuit I had brought with me.

From my research, I was expecting the water of Flathead Lake to be cold - it was still receiving snowmelt from the mountains until July. No way was I going to sit on the sidelines all summer merely watching the campers swim, so I purchased a second-hand Billabong wetsuit back home and resigned myself to some laughs for wearing it. On the contrary, the campers thought I was a cool Aussie surfer, although my image was somewhat diminished when I admitted that I had never surfed in my life.

A different age group of campers arrived each week, and it was fantastic to be in the midst of so many American young people again, playing in the great outdoors and teaching them more about Jesus and how to follow Him. Sketches, games and lots of singing helped them learn more from the Bible, and as well as having morning devotions at the outdoor chapel, every evening concluded with campfire vespers, our singing accompanying the glorious sunset as it filled the sky over the lake with rich colour.

After a couple of weeks, the thought of leaving before the end of the summer was quite upsetting. Two other staff also needed to leave camp before the end of the season due to other commitments. A shortage of three would create quite a staffing challenge for the last few weeks of camps.

Furthermore, after only a week at camp all that extra library-induced pain and tension had disappeared from my neck and shoulders. Despite the movement and activity that filled each camp day – climbing stairs to and from the log cabins and the lake; playing games; swimming and canoeing; hiking; ropes course – my muscles were experiencing only the fatigue and aches and pains of ME.

The difference in my pain levels was so marked that I feared returning to my job would have a long-term detrimental effect on my body. It seemed stupid to stay in a situation which would make my physical condition worse.

These thoughts were expressed to God in prayer and I waited for peace and confirmation about whether to resign from my library job.

However, a number of details over which I had no control had to work out if I was indeed to leave that job and thus stay at Glacier camp until the end of the summer. It was not as simple as merely resigning and I would need an answer from God very soon so the required notice to my library employer could be given if I decided to leave.

Firstly, the camp director had to want me to stay on. Then I would have to see if the dates of my three connecting flights could be changed and after that, my travel insurance had to be extended.

The camp director was more than happy that I stay until the end of the summer. My travel insurance could be extended simply by paying the top-up cost, which Mum and Dad would organise on my behalf.

QANTAS would change my flight date from LA–Brisbane at no charge, provided there were seats available. Only a few seats remained for the day I planned to leave so I was advised to make my decision quickly. Everything seemed to be falling into place and my excitement grew.

However, my heart sank during my phone call to Alaska Airlines to change my two domestic flights. My discount price tickets allowed no date changes at all and purchasing completely new tickets was not a viable option for me. Disappointed, I accepted that I would be returning to Australia as originally planned.

Upon explaining the situation, my camp director had no hesitation in offering that the camp pay for new domestic tickets as it would cost less than employing someone to fill my place for the rest of the summer. The possibility was alive again.

My employer had to be contacted on a couple of counts. Because of the physiotherapy I had been receiving through Workplace Health and Safety, I needed to ensure that I was under no obligation to stay until further procedures were followed. The answer was that I was free to leave, providing I was happy to absolve the Council of any further responsibility in that regard.

Well, that was it; all obstacles had been surmounted – all that was left to do was resign….by email…from the other side of the world. A concern was how this would be perceived by my boss, when I had been very appreciative of the job and all I had learnt over the previous six years. This was not a lightly-taken decision, nor did I intentionally wait until I was far away in Montana to resign.

I composed the email and paused for a few moments to pray before pressing 'send', realising that on doing so I would be free to stay longer in Montana, but that I would also be unemployed, with no idea what to do when I got home. Was I doing the right thing? God had worked out all those other details, and I had such peace in my heart without the nagging doubts I had when I wanted to leave my job prior to leaving Brisbane. Although I couldn't quite understand the timing difference, I would just have to take the risk and trust God that it would all work out. The email was sent and I turned my attention to plane tickets.

QANTAS booked me on only one of two remaining seats on the flight I requested. With the camp's credit card in hand, I phoned Alaska Airlines to buy new domestic tickets. Amazingly I was told that instead, my existing ticket could be taken to the airline counter at Kalispell airport where they would change my flight dates for only fifty US dollars! I was relieved that the camp wouldn't have to outlay so much, and that the money could be used for some other aspect of the ministry.

The response to my email to the library was a request that I postpone my resignation in the light of further discussion upon my return to Brisbane. What an unexpected blessing! Not only could I spend the rest of the summer at camp, but there was a possibility of staying at the library in some capacity. This unexpected – but very positive – outcome was more than I could have hoped for.

The weather did warm up somewhat as June progressed and although not *quite* like a Brisbane summer, I was eventually wearing shorts and t-shirts to bask each day in the sun, at least for a few weeks. The lake water, however, didn't ever warm up. The wetsuit meant I could swim or go 'blobbing' for about half an hour at a time before having to get out and defrost beneath the sun's rays on the warm dock. Blue lips don't do a thing for my complexion!

A camp tradition was the morning 'polar bear swim', for which the campers were loudly awakened before breakfast. The cacophony of various pots and pans nabbed from the kitchen was the signal to gather for an optional wake-up dip in the lake. The bravest of souls would line up along the dock in swimsuits (or wetsuit, as in my case), count to three, dive in and scramble out as quickly as possible to try to catch our breath.

The cold was so biting that it literally took our breath away and upon surfacing, the competition was keen to be the first to reach the ladder and climb out. I am proud to say that I was the only counsellor who did the polar bear swim every single morning – not bad at all for a girl from the tropics. There was definitely a dearth of Montanan counsellors present at those morning dips!

The pressure mounted for me to ditch the wetsuit and wear just my swimsuit like everybody else. In my head the answer was clearly 'Never!' Somehow, the bargain was struck that the wetsuit be retired on the first day of August. When the day came, the campers allowed me no option of chickening out. Oh, the anticipation of perching on the end of the Blob waiting to be catapulted off at any moment into the bone-chilling depths of the lake. The speed with which I swam back to the dock to get out of the water was record-breaking.

Daily it was obvious how ideally God had placed me at this camp of days filled with outdoor activities, gorgeous scenery, and plenty of scope to use my gifts, experience and passions. I was easily able to input creative ideas for Bible teaching and craft sessions and played my guitar and sang at campfire devotions.

The weeks varied in content and style – from day camp; to a half-week introductory camp where the youngest children came with a mum or dad; to upper primary weeks; to junior high weeks; to senior high conference; to specialty weeks such as Wet, Wild and Wacky camp and MAD (Music, Art and Drama) Camp; to 'Camp-In-A-Van', where a few staff went with the camp mini-van to other churches to run a day camp programme.

Nevertheless, camp was camp with its inevitable physical demands and long hours. Although my

From the Ends of the Earth

spirit soared, my body struggled with its limited energy resources. My body had improved somewhat in health since my last experience of summer camp, but I had come from working only part-time in a library to an almost 24/7 summer of camps. Once again, God's solution was not to physically heal me of ME, but to be faithful to supply all that I needed for each day. Energy didn't always overflow and some days I was so desperately tired and sore that I was close to tears, but other days were easier. Whatever my state, God enabled me to do the job I was called to do.

Although a little frustrated by missing out on some staff social occasions, my priority had been to come and share Jesus with campers, and I was able to do exactly that. Even when I had to sit out some of the more physical camp activities, I was treated with understanding by the other leaders, and also by the children, who showed great compassion and would often ask if I was okay. My physical weakness was often an entry into conversation with children who struggled to keep up with life in different areas, and as a springboard for spiritual discussions about how God gives me purpose in life and helps me through the difficult times.

Yet again God proved that His faithfulness in my weakness was a powerful message to others that could encourage them in their own walk with God or spark their interest in the Christian faith. Yet again He proved how ungrounded were my fears that illness would impair my potential in His service. In fact, the evidence showed that the opposite was true and that I need not fear what the future held.

Chapter 15

At the end of August 2000 I flew back to Brisbane and, after some recovery time, returned to work for some discussion with my employer. To my utter delight, the outcome was that I would continue working in the library, solely with Young People's Library Services. Rather than return home unemployed as I thought would be the case, I ended up with a job that was even better than before. Unbelievable!

My chief tasks would be preparation of craft activities for children aged four to sixteen for the library school holiday programme, leading craft sessions, storytelling for the younger age groups, and special projects should there be extra money available in the budget.

A more perfect job for me couldn't be imagined - working alongside a librarian and library technician whom I held in high esteem and with whom I had a great relationship; sitting at a desk next to a whole mini-library of craft books, and with a workbench on which to 'play' and create with the contents of cupboards full of craft materials; the responsibility of shopping (tough job but someone has to do it!) for supplies and keeping to an annual budget; and in school holiday time and at other regular times during the year, storytelling and crafts with children and teenagers. How could I wish for anything more?

The only downside was that initially I was guaranteed just one day of work each week. There would most likely be more, but possibly not on a regular basis. Long-term I needed to be earning a certain amount of money, but my body needed a gentle few months anyway, so why not see how things went?

After all, God knew all my needs. He knew that being a casual employee, although providing a higher hourly rate, would mean no paid annual or sick leave entitlements and a less regular income, but I received this job as a gift and trusted Him with the details.

I threw myself into my new job with gusto - cutting, gluing, colouring, experimenting, shopping and storytelling. My creativity could run wild, and ideas flowed. Sometimes it felt a bit like being at camp...except I could sleep peacefully in my own bed each night...and it seemed like a dream that I was actually earning money by having so much fun. Could I even call it 'work'?

Finances were taken care of. There always seemed to be money available at just the right time for extra work, and averaged over a fortnightly basis, I don't think I once earned less than I had as a part-time employee. Budgeting on my previous wage, the extra was squirreled away.

My health was noticeably improved. This job was nowhere near as physically demanding as my previous one, and my spirit and mind were nourished as I exercised my creative gifts.

The symptoms of ME didn't disappear but I felt better able to cope on bad days because I largely worked to my own timetable. It was generally up to me to decide how to meet the targets for different periods of the year. Therefore, on my bad days, I could choose to do more mundane tasks (yes, there were some, even in such a dream job) that didn't require much physical movement or brain work. Therefore, I could go home from work each day satisfied that I had been productive, which was a great psychological benefit.

As I beavered away at my workbench on the school holiday craft programme, a couple of extra projects added more variety to my job. One was to make a portable standing puppet theatre. Extra hours, some extra money, and loads of extra fun for me. Not only was I able to make it, I would get to use it also.

Is it any wonder I felt torn when a couple of months after starting my new job, I received an email from the director of Glacier Camp asking me to consider returning the following summer as the Programme Director?

What to do? I had come back from the States with as great a passion for the country as ever and a new-found love for beautiful Montana. However, to take this new position would mean four months off work, arriving a couple of weeks before the camps started to settle in and organise programme details, and leaving a couple of weeks after the summer to either finish up around the camp or visit some friends to relax and rest before coming home.

Although I wanted to grab this opportunity immediately, I was cautious, praying fervently that God would show me whether this was what *He* wanted me to do. After all, it seemed that He had provided this perfect library job for me; I found it hard to believe that the right thing would be to walk away from it so soon. I felt that I couldn't in good conscience ask for four months off work and expect to keep my job having had it so short a time and being only a casual employee. Besides, I would miss not only one, but two of the year's four school holiday periods – our busy time with storytelling and craft programmes and that wasn't fair to the library.

I wrestled with and prayed about the issue for days, finally deciding to mention the email offer from the camp to my boss, Jenny, and simply explain how I was feeling. I had always found Jen extremely approachable, trustworthy, understanding and fair and I would know from her honest response whether she thought I was being demanding or fickle in either seeking time off or resigning so soon. As a Christian, I took work commitments seriously whatever my job might be, and I would honour her response.

From the Ends of the Earth

My colleagues knew of my faith, and while I wasn't interested in putting on a good show for other people, I knew that my actions needed to square with the faith I professed. Messing my secular employer around unfairly just to do 'something for God' would not honour His Name. If Jen showed any sign of displeasure, I would drop the idea of returning to Montana and stay with the library, trusting that God would answer my prayers for direction through her response.

When I met with Jenny and nervously explained my situation, her response was spontaneous and genuine. Genuinely thrilled that I was being offered such a wonderful opportunity, she was willing to endorse four months' leave without pay. The request went to the Human Resources department for final approval.

I had my answer – God had made it plain, and was going to bless me with *both* opportunities (my leave request was approved). Overwhelmed at God's goodness, I was also very, very humbled. For all the years that I had been working part-time and struggling with illness since my first visit to the USA, I had had some rather frank conversations with God about how it seemed that my life was going nowhere while all my friends furthered their careers, travelled, married, had children, bought houses, etc, etc, etc. There I had been 'stuck' (as I saw it sometimes) in a job which, although it provided for my financial needs and which I did enjoy, was not what I studied five years at university for and which often didn't mentally challenge me. While I loved my parents deeply, I hadn't planned on living with them as my twenties slipped by and moved towards my thirties; and I was still single with no prospect of marriage and children on the horizon. All this and health which although stabilised over the previous years, was not getting me any closer to a 'full-time' life in any sphere – career-wise, socially or ministry-wise.

How little I understood of God's big picture of my life. He was able to see the scope of the whole life's plan He had for me – I could see only the past and the present. He knew what future positions and places for which He was preparing me, and the kind of experiences and trials I would need to walk through before I was ready and able to fulfil the potential He had placed in me. He knew the perfect times to position me in just the right places to meet the people who would inspire me and have positive input into my life, and those for whom I could do the same.

Apparently I was now ready to be sent around the globe at very short notice. God had certainly refined my faith and deepened my understanding of His character and ways so that all He had to do was say 'Go!', and I would go (literally) to the ends of the earth to do what He called me to do.

I emailed the camp in Montana to accept their offer, bought yet another airline ticket, and settled into advance preparation of the library winter and spring holiday programmes for which I would be absent. God was so faithful – ideas came, budget money stretched, and box after box was filled, labelled and stored under my workbench.

To the airport I returned in June 2001, eagerly anticipating another summer at Glacier Camp. Better prepared for the climate this time, my backpack contained thermal layers and warm polar fleeces alongside my wetsuit. What I didn't know was that this summer would be quite different from the previous one, and my faith and endurance was in for quite a workout.

The first hiccup occurred before I even arrived at camp. My flights were with a fairly new Canadian budget airline which provided by far the best price for my return ticket to Montana. I would fly Brisbane-Honolulu-Vancouver with them, and then switch to Alaskan Airlines for my Vancouver-Seattle-Kalispell flights.

Upon arrival in Honolulu, all passengers disembarked to wait in the transit lounge for the hour or so until it was time to reboard. One hour passed, then another, and another. Passengers were becoming hungry and grumpy – it was the middle of the night Hawaiian time and the trip was long and tiring enough as it was without delays in airports. No announcements about the problem or resumption of our journey were given and we weren't allowed to leave the transit lounge to walk around or find somewhere to sit and buy coffee or a snack.

As we waited, I overheard snatches of a conversation between two girls sitting nearby. The mention of an accompanying jar of Vegemite combined with a couple of other things made me certain that one of the girls was also on her way to an American summer camp. With no one else to talk to, I decided to chance a polite interruption to find out if this was the case.

In fact, both girls were off to camps in the States. The one I had overheard talking, Shirley, was a teenager from Sydney and the other was closer to my age. The two of them had met at Sydney airport. We exchanged information about our destinations and when I said that I was going to a Christian camp in Montana, Shirley's eyes lit up. She was going to a Christian camp, too! Of all the passengers there, God had led me to another Christian with whom I could pass the time.

As the transit lounge grew unbearably hot and stuffy, I noticed that sitting nearby was a young woman in her early twenties with a crying and restless baby. Feeling sorry for her plight, I and my two new friends started chatting to her, discovering she was a Canadian married to an Australian and taking her baby to meet his Canadian grandparents. The little boy was hungry and needed changing, but the airline attendants couldn't be persuaded to fill his bottle with water to mix more formula. No one seemed to know what was going on with our flight, and although we were eventually supplied with some small cartons of orange juice, tensions in the small room were increasing and sleep-deprived passengers were rapidly losing patience.

Six long hours passed before the pilot made an announcement over the loudspeaker. I kid you not; part of his spiel went like this, 'Ladies and gentlemen, thank you for your patience. I have good news and bad news. The good news is that you have been flying in a brand new plane which is only a few years old, and one of the newest in the fleet. The bad news is that there is a problem with one of the wing flaps, and because the plane is so new, replacement parts are quite scarce. We are currently searching the west coast of the USA for the right part, and we hope to be able to resume our journey within twenty-four hours.'

Good news and bad news indeed! You can imagine the various passenger responses. Although it was nobody's fault and it was certainly better to discover a fault with the plane's wing while we were on the ground, exhaustion fought with my determination to keep a godly attitude. At least I had three new friends, and could help with the baby. Tired, hot and sleepless was one thing for me to deal with - imagine coping with a baby as well.

Finally, the information was disseminated that we would be bussed out of the airport and to hotels in Waikiki. Officially entering the USA meant that first all our luggage had to be collected and immigration forms completed. By this stage it was dawn and we were starving, having had no food for about eight hours.

As we trudged wearily towards baggage claim, I noticed a tiny elderly woman walking along with the crowd, looking a bit lost. I stopped to help her and she gratefully held onto my arm. She was worried about managing her heavy suitcases as her son had put her on the plane in Sydney and she hadn't counted on having to deal with her luggage until her arrival in Canada.

I was able to lift her bags off the carousel and help her fill out the immigration forms. Worried about the stern expression on the faces of some of the immigration officials, she asked if I could go with her when she was called forward; 'After all, you could be my daughter!' she said.

The immigration process completed, we were at last standing in the warm, humid morning air of Honolulu, awaiting buses. Unfortunately, I was dressed warmly for the plane and for my arrival in Montana, and not for weather that rivalled Brisbane's summer heat! I had regrouped with my three friends and the baby so we could go to the same hotel. An hour later, the buses finally arrived and we gratefully boarded.

At the Waikiki Marriot Hotel, Shirley asked me if we could share a room; I was happy to oblige. The other two girls shared a room nearby, and after dumping our luggage, we were finally fed in the hotel's dining room. Buses would collect us at about midnight to return us to the airport.

After a heavenly shower and change of clothes, and feeling much refreshed after food, hot water, and the daylight, none of us felt inclined to sleep. We were in Hawaii after all – we might as well see some of it – why not catch a bus into town and do some shopping?! And thus four girls and baby Sam (and his pram) spent the day hopping on and off buses, exploring our unexpected stopover destination. Is it any wonder God had been teaching me over the last few years to be more flexible, to stress less, and to be more on the lookout for the comfort of others than to be concerned with the mess-up of my own agenda?

Back at the hotel by 6.00pm for some dinner it was time to try to snatch a few hours' sleep. In our room, Shirley and I chatted some more and spent time praying together for our separate summers at camp and for the rest of our journey. This was not quite the way I had envisaged visiting Hawaii, I have to say, but then again, here I was in the Marriot Hotel, praying with another Christian I had known less than a day, encouraging her and being encouraged by her.

Although Shirley managed to fall asleep I couldn't, and as we would have to be up in another few hours anyway, I joined one of the other girls for a walk along the beachfront. A moonlit walk by the ocean on Waikiki Beach – it could have been quite romantic in other circumstances! I had to smile though – here I was adding another American State to add to the list of places I had visited. God and His sense of humour…honestly, you couldn't make this up.

Back at the airport, the whole check-in process was repeated and followed by a couple of hours waiting to board our plane. I really don't know how I would have coped with this whole situation had it not been for the company of the girls, and I think they felt the same way. On my own, I would have cried with frustration and fatigue but instead, God had provided a way to make it bearable, even fun. We giggled at the picture we must have painted just then – sprawled out and lying on our bags on the airport floor, the baby in the middle! When you're this tired, who cares what you look like?

I eventually made it to Montana, and although utterly exhausted, was immediately refreshed and blessed by the sight of the lake and the mountains. How good it was to be back.

From the Ends of the Earth

During the first couple of weeks there was plenty to do between preparing various aspects of the camp programme and doing some maintenance around the site. My work at the library had perfectly prepared me with loads of tried and tested ideas for the summer craft programme, and of course my shopping skills came in handy here, too. My skill base expanded as I helped build an equipment shed near the ropes course – I was pretty proud of that achievement, although all I really did was hammer nails and hold wood when I was told to.

The three of us doing pre-summer preparations were invited to a dinner one evening at a neighbouring Christian camp to meet their staff and some of the local residents. It was there I was introduced to Eugene Peterson, author of 'The Message' version of the Bible and a long list of Christian books which have helped me greatly in my faith. You just never know who you might meet when you go where God leads!

About half the camp counsellors were returnees from the previous year, but I was fulfilling a very different role this time. Although I felt honoured to have this new leadership responsibility, it was initially a little difficult not to have a group of my own campers each week to befriend and nurture. It was useful to think in terms of the counselors being my 'campers' for the summer, my primary responsibility being to care for them as well as to co-ordinate their work. A Portuguese girl in her late twenties joined our team this year and I enjoyed helping her settle in to the American culture and language.

A highlight was renewing relationships with campers (and some of their parents) from the previous summer. My new role did not exclude my playing on the Blob or the morning polar bear swims in my wetsuit. I eagerly fulfilled the responsibility of raucous wake-up calls with pots and pans filched from the kitchen. Playing my guitar and helping with the Bible teaching times continued as well.

The joy of camp was tempered with an unexpected amount of pressure. A number of issues made for a difficult time of ministry and in my position of leadership, I felt the strain tremendously. Providing balanced spiritual guidance and keeping up morale took every ounce of energy I had (and a lot that I felt I didn't have), and I wondered how I would last the distance. I didn't understand all that was going on, but God had definitely placed me here and so I just had to keep going. I continued my early morning quiet times overlooking the lake, and arose early to read and pray for a lengthy time each morning before anyone else was up. Giving this extra time and energy to God gave me the strength I needed for each day – spiritually, physically, mentally and emotionally. Leadership lessons abounded, especially regarding endurance under pressure.

Despite the stresses, God gave relief in different ways – through the encouragement of many of the counsellors, little gifts from campers, and the friendship and prayers of friends I had met the previous year. There were many bright points in the summer, especially helping the campers in their spiritual growth, or hearing them sing and pray. This was what it was all about and I was so glad to be there.

Once again, God arranged unexpected travel experiences. My current boss and John were to construct a climbing wall at a camp near Seattle, Washington. Tagging along for the ride, Sandra (the Portuguese girl) and I enjoyed a few days' break at this beautiful campsite. Greatly refreshed by walking, talking and lounging around in the sun, we justified our presence as official testers of the climbing wall. (It passed!)

The parents of one of the Glacier Camp counsellors owned a cottage on the shores of Lake Coeur D'Alene in Idaho. It proved the perfect get-away for a few days off, with most of the staff camping out on the front lawn overnight. Tubing on the lake behind a speedboat was an ideal stress- buster (once I learned the art of hanging on).

At the end of the camp season, I was utterly exhausted and badly needed some recuperation time before I flew home. God graciously filled my final weeks with visits to friends who cared for me, including some camp friends in Missoula and John and Fay, who had moved to a Christian camp in Idaho.

There was no better medicine for me at this point than to be surrounded by their love and the hustle and bustle of their home. Due to fly out of the USA on September 16, I had planned to stay with them until a few days before. I then would spend a couple of days with my friend Sandy (the Glacier Camp cook) in Kalispell before flying home.

Of course, everything changed on the morning of September 11. We sat glued to the television, watching in utter disbelief as the first of the twin towers of the World Trade Centre collapsed and fell to the ground, the second tower falling only moments later. Looking like something out of a science fiction movie, we struggled to believe it was really happening right at that moment. I had stood on the observation deck of the World Trade Centre only seven years earlier, admiring the amazing views of New York. Now all that was left was a flaming pile of rubble.

Indescribable shock and horror swept across the country in the subsequent days. I didn't know how or when I would get home considering the growing backlog of hundreds of flights across the country and internationally, but that hardly seemed important in the grand scale of the tragedy.

From the Ends of the Earth

I accompanied Fay to a special prayer meeting at their church. After a long time of prayer focusing on the tragedy at hand, the group then spent some time praying for me – particularly for my health and safety in travel home. I was touched when they all gathered around my chair and laid hands on my shoulders. I was completely worn out, not only physically after such a period of activity, but also emotionally and spiritually after the leadership strains of the summer. I had followed God's calling to come to camp again, and although I had made mistakes, I had done the best I knew how in the situation. John and Fay did not know the details – they knew only that it had been hard going.

As these people prayed and shared words of encouragement, a huge burden felt lifted from my shoulders. Through the words of others, God was assuring me that He had seen and understood everything, and that He was pleased with my service.

God also had some things to say about the future, although I wouldn't understand it all just then. Fay's hands moved from my shoulders to touch my feet, and she prayed for blessing and protection upon me as I continued to go wherever God called me to go with the gospel, and for safe flights home this week.

After our prayer time, while chatting and answering some questions about myself (after all, these people had never met me before), one of the men suddenly said that a picture had just come to his mind of a jumbo jet flying from east to west, and he said to me 'Go, go, go!' The image didn't strike a chord with me at that point at all. After all, I wasn't planning any trips for the near future, and besides, flying from east to west was going in the opposite direction from Australia to the USA, and flying west to east was my preferred option. Fay glanced my way and smiled; I knew she was thinking the same thing.

My major concern now was getting home. Flights were gradually resuming across the country after two days of none at all, but the backlog of stranded passengers and disrupted flight schedules was staggering. It would take weeks to catch up. The only advice airlines could give was to phone each day to check which flights were going ahead.

This was easier said than done, however, as I needed three internal flights plus my international flight to connect. I was flying Kalispell-Missoula then Missoula-Seattle then Seattle-Vancouver then Vancouver-Honolulu-Brisbane. Suddenly, that twenty-four hour delay on my flight to the USA a few months ago seemed like no big deal at all.

In Kalispell I stayed with Sandy as originally planned. Welcome to stay with her as long as I needed, she would drive me to the airport when I was able to depart. Even so, I felt 'antsy' not knowing when that would be. Although I knew that Jen would hardly mind if I was late back to work in such circumstances, I was not keen on this idea considering the lengthy time off I'd been granted.

Each day I phoned the airlines – sometimes one or two of my flights would be scheduled to go ahead, but the other/s wouldn't, which was no good to me. I couldn't afford to be stranded for days in another city, and would just have to stay where I was until all my flights connected. Even when they did, there would be some risk involved once I left Kalispell, as flights were being cancelled at a moment's notice if any suspicious circumstances arose.

Finally, on September 18, the airlines confirmed all my flights were scheduled to go ahead. At Kalispell airport I checked in with the crowd of passengers, many of whom made no secret of the fact that they were disgruntled and frustrated with the travel delays they had experienced. Airport security was intense, and the terminals were a hotbed of emotion and tension. The counter staff had my sympathies as they bore the brunt of angry words and explosive tempers. An example was occurring right in front of me as a passenger's frustration overflowed.

My tongue hurt with the effort of biting it - I honestly felt like telling the man to shut up and recognise that his inconvenience was nothing compared with the pain of those who had lost loved ones in this whole mess. All I could do was keep that fact to the fore of my own mind as I walked on the edge of frustration and weariness myself.

The testing process of check-in over, I waited at my departure gate for the boarding announcement, coffee and a book in hand. Wariness was my initial response when this very man approached but to my surprise, he apologised for his earlier behaviour. Although feeling too tired to talk, I forced myself to be polite. It turned out that he was a Christian whose teenage son had just begun a course at the nearby Youth With a Mission base. Personal stresses added to the repercussions of the World Trade Center tragedy had stretched him to breaking point. I accepted the apology for his impatient behaviour. Noticing my accent, he wondered what I was doing in Montana. Upon hearing that I was a Christian involved in ministry too, he relaxed and said that it was just the encouragement he needed to calm down and get some perspective. God at work again.

At long last the boarding announcement came, but no sooner had we lined up than the flight was abruptly cancelled. My heart sank as I calculated how the delay would affect my next two flights. I would arrive in Seattle after my flight to Vancouver was due to depart and I didn't know if they would hold the flight or go ahead and try to clear some of the backlog of passengers, putting me on the following flight. In the latter case, I would miss my flight to Brisbane. I couldn't bear the thought of being stuck in an airport for a couple of days as the airline only flew to Brisbane three times a week.

From the Ends of the Earth

Worrying would achieve nothing – I was checked in and so was my baggage. The journey would have to continue as I trusted God that everything would work out. Although feeling a little anxious, I was glad that all of my emotion could be turned over to God in prayer, and that I could trust in Someone who was greater than my circumstances. Besides, I now had a Christian travelling companion who, despite first impressions, was turning out to be pleasant company and who was praying too. It was comforting to discover that the flight's cancellation was due to a glitch discovered by a safety check, and not related to terrorist activity or suspicious circumstances.

I was subsequently asked by people if I was afraid to be flying so soon after September 11 and I can honestly say that I felt no trepidation in the face of the travel ahead. Don't get me wrong - I didn't relish dying in a plane crash or a hijacking and the delays had exhausted and frustrated me, but I felt no panic or even nervousness at the thought of stepping onto a plane and spending hours flying or waiting in airports. I knew that my life was in God's hands and I could not die before God had ordained the time for my life to be over. If that was to be this day, so be it – I was ready to meet Him with my eternal destiny in heaven assured; and if not, I had nothing to fear because I knew He would protect me. Peace governed my soul, and it was comforting to know that my family felt the same peace although there were still natural twinges of anxiety until my feet landed safely back on Australian soil.

Thankfully, the next flight from Kalispell went ahead as scheduled. Hurrying off the plane and running to the departures board I found that my next flight had been delayed just long enough for me to catch it....*but* it was due into Vancouver the same time my flight to Brisbane was due out, and I had to collect my baggage and go through Canadian immigration in between. Oh well, forward was the only direction now!

In Vancouver I discovered that my flight to Brisbane had been delayed two hours –enough time to collect my baggage, clear immigration, check into my international flight, and even make quick phone calls to a couple of American friends to tell them I was safe and almost on my way home. In the crowded departure lounge I overheard one guy with a leg encased in plaster say he had spent the last two days in the airport without money to stay in a hotel besides which most places were booked out anyway. I don't know how my health and sanity would have coped with that after everything else and I was so thankful that God had delivered me to this point with nothing more serious than a few delays. Even my baggage had managed to arrive with me. Proof again that God knows just how much I can take, and cares for me in every situation.

From the Ends of the Earth

As the plane climbed its way high above the ocean on the way back to Brisbane, mixed emotions flooded over me – memories of the summer encompassed difficulties in ministry but also many treasured moments with campers, staff and close friends. I had God's assurance and encouragement about those things that I didn't understand, and peace that although I had made mistakes, I had done my best and learnt many lessons.

Woven through these thoughts seemed to be the message that God was 'closing the door' on the United States. Although not what I wanted to hear, I knew that His future plans and purposes for me were, by His nature, good; but still I mourned flying away from this country that I had so loved and felt called to, not knowing when, if ever, I would return. It wasn't clear whether God was saying that I would never be back, or whether the door was closed just for a season of my life. That was not for me to know now.

To my mind just then came a vivid image. I saw a clear picture of a sword being brandished, the steel of its blade flashing in the light. It spoke of God's assurance that as a result of the difficult leadership challenges of the summer there was a flash of 'steel' in me that hadn't been there before. Not a callous hardness, but a steel of determination, and a steel of strength in my character and spiritual life that only the endurance of fiery tests can develop. At the time I felt I had as much strength and steel as a washed out dishrag, but I was encouraged to think that this might be a glimpse of what God had accomplished in my life and that I would see the benefits one day. All I wanted to do now was to go home and catch up on a whole lot of sleep; the rest could wait.

From the Ends of the Earth

Chapter 16

On September 20, 2001, I was in Australia once again. I returned to my library job, enormously grateful for the extended leave I had been allowed, but still with a burning desire to travel and do more mission work in the future. As a casual employee I was given four weeks' unpaid annual leave each year, and I immediately dedicated my next year's holiday time to God. He would just have to point me in the right direction and draw my attention to the right opportunity, and I would be ready to go.

Over the next few months, I started searching for possibilities. It seemed unreasonable to request more than my four weeks' entitlement this time. My Christian witness was at stake and I didn't want to create the impression that I was 'milking' my employers for all I could get out, focusing more on holidays than on my job. That wasn't what my attitude actually was and I was anxious that it not even slightly appear that way.

Sometimes God's call comes clearly and quickly as it did in the case of Romania. Sometimes, however, His guidance comes through information or people that we come across; it's not a matter of waiting passively for God to shout directions from above.

I set to working exploring avenues that came to mind - Mission Without Borders regarding a possible return to Romania; a Christian friend from university living in Namibia; a school friend in ministry in Botswana; and a mission programme in England I had heard about. Many lunch breaks at work were spent surfing the net for web pages of various mission organisations. Although it felt odd not to be considering the USA for opportunities, I didn't even bother to look in that direction – there was no point. If God was saying that door was closed, I wasn't about to force it open.

Finding a mission opportunity began to consume my thoughts, and I became frustrated that it all seemed like hard work this time, in comparison with the previous three years when God had spoken to me so clearly. One lunchtime at work, as I tapped away at the computer for more internet searches, the words 'Hands Off!' came clearly to mind - so clearly, in fact, that I lifted my hands off the keyboard immediately and sat back in my chair!

A Christian friend, after hearing me voice my frustrations, asked if perhaps God wanted me to stay in Australia this year. My problem was that I had become so used to 'going places' for God in my holidays that although I had given Him my next year's annual leave (with good motivation), I hadn't actually asked Him whether He wanted me to go anywhere at all. At the thought that He might actually be asking me to stay at home for the next twelve months or more, my first mental response was, 'Oh, no, God – please don't!'

Surprised by the intensity of that feeling, I proceeded to sincerely examine my motives. Why did I so fervently want to 'go' again this year? Was it because God was actually calling me, or was I trying to fulfil some other need? Did I subconsciously perceive my mission work as a way of proving to myself and others that I was doing something 'useful' with my life, in the absence of being able to live the kind of life my peers did? I had largely come to grips with the life I was leading, being thankful for all that I *could* do, but it was amazing the subtle ways in which the old 'comparison' habit would rear its ugly head.

Complete surrender of my own plans and ideas to God was the key, asking Him to clearly reveal how *He* wanted me to spend my holidays, with my whole heart willing to obey whatever He asked, wherever and whenever.

Once my own agenda had been abandoned, it wasn't long before I was sure that God *did* want me to do some more overseas mission work – I just had to discover where. God doesn't make His will elusive, even though it may seem a bit of a puzzle at first. One by one, as I looked at the opportunities I had collected thus far, He seemed to cross them off the list for various reasons.

Kathryn Kerridge

MWB's next volunteer trip to Romania was scheduled during dates when the library young people's holiday activities were in full swing. I had already decided that in good conscience I could not go away over the school holiday period again as that was a focal point of my job and an extremely busy time for YPLS.

My friend in Namibia emailed to say that there were a number of things she could arrange for me to do in conjunction with her church, as well as possible work with SU. Despite her positive response, my strong impression as I read her email was that Namibia (or any part of Africa for that matter) wasn't the place to go. Therefore, I no longer pursued my friends in Botswana for opportunities. The English organisation had emailed to say that they would only accept people under the age of twenty-six for their programme – no exceptions, so I crossed that one off my list as well. Another mission programme based in the south of England had caught my interest, but after repeatedly emailing them and receiving no response, I forsook that idea as well.

My investigations led to one dead end after another. Resignedly I thought that if nothing else worked out, I could at least go back and do a camp or two in Scotland with SU, interspersed with some travel. I was still in touch with a couple of my campers from Lendrick Muir in 1999, as well as one of the leaders who lived in Glasgow. Being on the SU Scotland mailing list since that camp, I regularly received their

From the Ends of the Earth

news magazine, prayer bulletins, and camp brochures. Although interested in the work, my connection was relatively remote - I hadn't met any SU staff during my visit, nor did I know much about the regions of Scotland in which they worked.

On the internet yet again during a work lunch break, I browsed the SU Scotland web site for their latest news. I'm not sure how I came across their 'gap year' link – I didn't even know there was a volunteer gap year programme and I certainly wasn't looking for a year-long mission opportunity. Nonetheless, I found myself drawn to read about the 'Year Team' options. I printed out the pages and at home added them to my pile of possible opportunities. As the other options were weeded out one by one eventually all that was left was the Year Team information. While no doubt interesting and worthwhile, it really was an absurd proposition as far as I was concerned.

Firstly, it was a whole year long, for goodness' sake! True, God had been lengthening my mission trips over the last few years, building my faith step by step as I pushed my body each time – two months, then three months, then four months – but a whole *year* of ministry? I wasn't ignorant concerning the task; several friends were or had been SU Queensland schools' workers. Crazy hours, a lot of time and energy spent travelling, and a heavy load of Christian leadership responsibility seemed par for the course – and none of these seemed compatible with my health condition.

Actually, I had been approached several times by SU Queensland staff during my decade of volunteering to consider working there, and yet it never seemed 'right', even though it would have made perfect sense considering my gifts and experience. Why would I go all the way to Scotland and pay a lot of money to do something for which I could stay at home and do as a paid job? It didn't make sense!

Besides, why Scotland anyway? I had never felt a particular affinity, love or calling for that country as I had the United States for most of my life. It just seemed an odd place to direct me to – it wasn't even as if I had any family connections there. If there was any place other than Australia in which I thought I would spend an extended period, it was the USA, and yet God had firmly closed the door on that. Still coming to grips with what seemed to me an abrupt change in direction, the whole idea of Scotland as a destination seemed nothing short of random.

Continuing down my list of objections (Moses wasn't the only one with a long list of 'valid' excuses!)...The cost was prohibitive, to say the least. Just to participate in the 'Schools' Plus' option entailed several thousand British pounds and the Australian dollar was at that time worth only about a third of the pound. In addition, I would need thousands more Australian dollars to cover airfares, travel insurance, shipping costs and the purchase of warm clothes and shoes for such a cold and wet climate, plus other inevitable extras.

From the Ends of the Earth

My objections continued. I was thirty-one years old. Surely gap year programmes targeted school or university leavers who wanted a year out before further study or work – I would be almost twice the age of some of the team. Surely that would be a bit odd?

As I perused the questions on the application form dealing with previous experience and use of gifts, I mentally ticked every single box. A decade's worth of leadership experience and children's ministry with SU Queensland, my church, and my library jobs could be listed. I certainly didn't regard myself as 'too good' for the programme. I was willing to do whatever God called me to do, but if the aim of Year Team was to provide experience to young people exploring ministry, helping them to discover their gifts and how to use them, I couldn't quite see how this was the best place for me to be at this point in my life - God had already given me a multitude of experiences which had achieved those aims.

Furthermore, going away for a year would mean resigning my wonderful job with YPLS which I had had for only eighteen months. I had waited years for something which was so tailored for my gifts and experience, and now I had a job that I loved so much I often couldn't believe I was being paid to do it. The responsibility I was given had became moulded around my gifts and experience so the job felt truly tailor-made by this point. Surely God didn't intend me to walk away from what He had so perfectly presented to me such a short time before.

Reasonable as all these objections seemed, January progressed but the notion of the gap year refused to budge from my mind. Strangely, I even found myself unable to rip up the information I had printed out and toss it in the bin. After a few weeks of this insistence within, I concluded that if there was the remotest possibility that God was prompting me to apply, I dare not disobey and should at least sit down and fill out the nine page form. I was reminded of the application process to go to the USA in 1994 – maybe the same thing was happening again in that I had to begin filling out the form in order to discern whether it was right or not. Maybe by the time I was halfway through I would decide it wasn't the right thing after all. In that case I'd have lost nothing, and I'd have to explain nothing as I hadn't yet shared my thoughts with another person, not even my parents.

Page after page of the form was completed, including disclosure of my medical condition, with an explanation of how ME affected my lifestyle generally, as well as how I had coped with short-term missions in the past. Oh well, I thought, let SU Scotland make of that what they will. That issue alone would be ample reason to reject my application (if I sent it in), and I would take that as God's answer.

The completed application form sat on my desk for a while until I became convinced that I *must* send it in. The next step was to approach Jen at the library, both to ask her for a reference and to warn her of my impending resignation. I wanted to allow as much time as possible for my position to be filled before I left.

While mulling the Year Team application over in my mind during these weeks, something remarkable had been happening with my work. Ideas for craft ideas and themes for holiday activities had been coming so thick and fast since my return from Montana that within a short time, I was working six months in advance. Crafts were prepared and boxed for school holidays way into the next financial year. Even more amazing was that all the necessary materials were being purchased from the current financial year's budget. My brain was working at a feverish pace, and I couldn't seem to spend the money fast enough.

Periods of creative inspiration and manic activity were not entirely new sensations to me either in work or in leisure, but this was something else...I would be able to approach Jen about the Year Team application together with the information that on my departure, the next twelve months of YPLS holiday activities would be completed. God, too, was concerned that it not seem that I was taking my job for granted. He understood the impact my departure would have on YPLS and was clearly undertaking for it.

Plane tickets had been another avenue of investigation. I made phone calls, scoured travel pages in newspapers and asked for quotes from my trusty travel agent ('Where to this time?!'). However, every time I looked at return travel fares, I had a distinctly uneasy feeling that it just 'wasn't right'. What? If God was leading me to Scotland and yet buying a return plane ticket didn't give me peace, what was going on? Surely not a one-way ticket? That was crazy! Well, not all that crazy, I guess, considering the rest of this whole idea.

It might have been a crazy idea, but at least it was a *possible* crazy idea! All because of that little 'Right of Abode to the UK' certificate already pasted in my passport, I needed no visa to spend a year in Scotland, and could indeed enter the country on a one-way plane ticket. No wonder I had felt prompted by God to get that sorted while I was preparing for my trip to Romania. It seemed that God had planned all along that I should return to Scotland, but I would still have to wait and see what became of my application after I had sent it in.

I prayed hard for the right time and opportunity to approach Jen at work and one quiet Friday afternoon I found myself in her office explaining my situation. After an immediate response of congratulations on such a wonderful opportunity, I was assured that she would have no hesitation in being a referee for me. Furthermore, she said that I would not necessarily need to resign – she would be happy to recommend

From the Ends of the Earth

to Human Resources that I be given a year's leave with the option of returning to my job afterwards. This was despite the fact that I was considering a one-way ticket and that I couldn't make a firm commitment to return as I honestly didn't know what the end of the year would bring.

My jaw quite literally dropped – I couldn't believe that I was being put in such a privileged position. As I walked out the door, it was as if God was reassuring me that I had nothing to lose – I still had a wonderful job if SU Scotland turned down my application, and I had a job to return to if SU accepted me and I came back after a year. There was no further reason to delay sending in my Year Team application. My church minister and another friend who worked for SU Queensland had also agreed to be referees for me and on March 18 my application was posted.

As I awaited the outcome, some regular mailings from SU Scotland arrived. Everything received from SU Scotland was scoured in a whole new light now, and I re-read some old newsletters to familiarise myself with the staff and variety of ministries.

Very noticeable was the number of regional staff vacancies that were highlighted. One in particular had been vacant for a very long time, and was mentioned in the prayer news, the SU magazine, and even a separate flyer. The message could not be ignored and I wondered if maybe God was sending me to Scotland for the purpose of becoming a regional staff worker in one of these places. A close Christian friend who also had a strong calling to overseas mission work listened to my thoughts. She took one look at the vacancy information and said that maybe that was my job!

I tentatively mentioned to her that I was wondering whether I should email SU Scotland to ask that my Year Team application be forwarded to the regional activities department, or whether I should just wait and mention it in passing when they contacted me about an interview. She encouraged me to go ahead and act in faith if I felt that strongly about it, and not to be airy-fairy. What did I have to lose?

Making contact with this reason would also be an opportunity to enquire about my application, as many weeks had passed and I still had no word about an interview. I requested that my application be passed on to the regional workers' department, feeling a bit ridiculous as I pressed the 'send' email button. Surely they would be wondering who on earth was this random Australian who sends in a gap year application and then asks about a job. Oh well, it wasn't as if my original Year Team application was entirely conventional anyway – all they could do was say 'no'.

The weeks of waiting time had me vacillating between certainty that I would be going to Scotland, and embarrassment about the lunacy of even applying. Patience was never my strongest virtue. I'm a forward planner who prefers to know well in advance what's in store so being in the dark for any length of time is always a test. However, faith by its nature requires patience, and all I could do was stay close to God, gain strength from His Word, and keep praying for His Will to be done, trusting that whatever that was, it was for my best.

One day at work, a new book caught my eye. Its subject matter was the lands of the Bible and the introductory page quoted words from Genesis 12:1 – *'The Lord had said to Abram, "Leave your native country, your relatives and your father's family, and go to the land that I will show you.'* (NLT). On the following page were some sentences about Abram being a traveller called to go to a foreign land, simply having to trust to God what would happen when he arrived. Was that what God was asking me to do, too, I wondered, leaving everything I knew for I don't know what, where or for how long?

I was finally interviewed for Year Team through the SU Queensland office by the staff worker who had given me the contact details which led me to camp in Scotland in 1999. As it turned out, he knew two key staff of SU Scotland who were involved in the administration and recruitment of the Year Team programme. Furthermore, one was on the management team of the organisation. Coincidence? I don't think so!

The results of the interview were relayed to SU Scotland, after which I received a phone call informing me of acceptance into the programme. My health situation, my age, and my previous experience had not been the barriers I feared. No further news about my application in regard to the job vacancies came, but that was fine – Year Team was what I had applied to do in the first instance, and God was making it plain that was the position for me.

God had cleared the way for me to go and spend a year in Scotland. For years, I had been saving money for the house/car I dreamed of having one day, and so I had the funds to pay for the year. I clearly felt God saying that He had given me the resources and this was how He wanted them used.

No good excuse remained, so with only a couple of months left before I was to leave the country, I bought a one-way plane ticket, shipped two big boxes of clothes, shoes, resources etc to the UK (which was cheaper than buying those items there), and commenced informing people of my plans and saying farewell to friends.

The news was met with various reactions – from concern about my health, to excitement about the opportunity, to the odd raised eyebrow (which I could completely understand). After all, the only information I had was that I would be spending a year in Scotland – I didn't know the town or city in which I would be based; nor the name of the schools' worker who would supervise me; nor the person with whom I would be living. In fact, there was far more that I *didn't* know about the year ahead than what I *did* know. No wonder people thought I was mad! The concept had been cooking in my mind for so many months by this stage that I had forgotten how strange it must have seemed to everyone else. However, I firmly believed God had engineered the opportunity, called me to go, and would take care of every detail, just as He did with Abram thousands of years ago. Different era; same God.

Besides, I had been praying about all the particulars for a long time. I prayed for a supervisor who understood my illness and would accept my limitations; for accommodation in a home which would allow me the necessary peace and personal space; for easy access to public transport as I wouldn't have a car - that maybe I could even borrow a bike; that I would be able to find a good church quickly; that I would find friends....there were so many 'unknowns' that I was completely depending on God to deal with in order for me to cope with the year well - physically, mentally, emotionally and spiritually.

Two weeks before my departure, a phone call came from the SU Scotland regional worker for Glasgow and Argyll, Fiona, to say that I would be working with her for the year and living in Glasgow. She sounded so bright and bubbly on the phone – I liked her immediately. One of the first things Fiona said was not to worry about my health – the previous year her Year Team person had a chronic illness, too, so she was not fazed about having to deal with mine. I was reminded of a saying I once heard – 'Do not worry about tomorrow; the Lord is already there.'

From the Ends of the Earth

Chapter 17

On August 9, 2002, Brisbane Airport once again played host to a gathering of my family and friends as I waited to board my flight. As I looked around the circle, I realised that God had gathered together significant Christian friends from each part of my life to be there in addition to my ever-faithful parents. There were two friends from primary school plus another from high school, my prayer partner from university, a friend with whom I had been a leader on several SU camps, and one of my former primary school campers who had just finished high school. It was very significant to have all these friends from different periods of my life and different parts of Brisbane together in one place, along with my wonderful Mum and Dad. I knew full well that with this one-way ticket, I didn't know exactly when I would see them again.

As the wearying thirty-six hour journey to Scotland commenced, I recalled my last summer in the USA and the prayer meeting I had attended with Fay. My feet were indeed carrying me to a different part of the world on God's work, and I was indeed in a jumbo jet flying east to west, as one man there had envisioned. I hadn't thought about the incident since, but God now brought it back to my mind as reassurance that He had planned all of this far in advance. There was therefore no cause for worry or fear.

I arrived in Glasgow as ready as I could be for the year ahead, but the dramatic climate change literally took my breath away. I had departed Brisbane on a sunny winter's day of twenty-four degrees Celsius....and arrived in Scotland during their 'warmest' month on a rainy, nippy day of sixteen degrees! I used to do a sports camp with SU Queensland in the middle of winter, and we could be running around outside in shorts and t-shirts in the middle of the day; heck, the bravest of us even went swimming in the ocean. Oh my, I thought, if *this* is summer (and I was chilled to the bone) what on *earth* would winter be like? A temperature of zero degrees was completely beyond my imagination, but not for long.

I quickly gained renown as the Aussie who was always cold. Wearing thermal layers and thick fleeces while the hardy natives walked around in sleeveless tops, shorts and summer dresses made me the subject of much hilarity, not an entirely new sensation to me by this stage.

At least God had prepared me somewhat by sending me to Montana for two summers in which I had spent the first month bundled up in my Australian winter clothes as the snow melted from the Mission Mountains into Flathead Lake. My wetsuit had accompanied me to Scotland, but I doubted very

From the Ends of the Earth

much that I would be swimming in *any* lochs or oceans here, at *any* time of year, wetsuit or not!

A couple of days after my arrival in Glasgow, I met with Fiona in the SU Scotland office in the city. A huge smile and a bear hug accompanied her genial greeting, and we talked effortlessly over lunch as if we'd known each other for years.

Fiona remarked that my application form reminded her a lot of herself – as it turned out, we were just under a year apart in age, and had both studied French and Law at university (at the same time on opposite sides of the world). We both played guitar, relished the creative arts, and even came from similar family situations – with our parents and one younger brother each. I was amazed at God's attention to detail. Furthermore, Fiona had travelled to Australia and understood some of my struggles with cultural and climate differences. A sympathetic listener, she would be a huge help during my homesick periods. God knew that I would need a colleague this year who could also fill the role of good friend and confidante; in Fiona He had made an excellent choice.

For the first four months I stayed with another SU staff worker in Glasgow. Libby was similar in age to myself and lived in a typical sandstone tenement flat in the east end of the city.

Kathryn Kerridge

The spare bedroom into which I settled had bright sunny yellow walls. Libby apologised for the 'loudness' of the colour – she intended to repaint it one day – but for me it was perfect. It was light and bright and reminded me of home, and together with the blue, white and yellow duvet cover, the colour combination was similar to my bedroom back home in Australia. You can't tell me God doesn't care about the little things!

The flat was opposite a train station, on several major city bus routes, and only a half-hour walk from the city centre. I would barely miss having a car at all. I could live quite independently, buying and cooking my own food, coming and going as I wished, and yet have the friendship and company of a flatmate of similar age. Answers to months of prayer were being clearly revealed – I remember going to bed astounded night after night at evidence of God's grace and generosity.

The climate, culture and accents made for an intense transition. I was sure the young people in the east end of Glasgow spoke a different language from the rest of Scotland. I was easily understood thanks to the popularity of 'Neighbours' and 'Home and Away' on television, but I often had to ask people to repeat what they were saying. And to think I had thought that at least God was sending me to another English-speaking country where I wouldn't have to learn a foreign language! Months of 'immersion' later, my ear finally became attuned to the Glaswegian accent and idiom.

In the first few weeks, I met with a number of local church ministers supportive of the ministry of SU. Due to my experience with children and young people, I was able to settle into work largely on my own, freeing Fiona for other aspects of her wide remit. No longer did it seem silly to be doing Year Team in Scotland at my age and stage in life, but rather a part of God's perfect planning to use me to assist Fiona in her ministry.

After visits to various churches, I felt at peace about committing to a Church of Scotland in the east end, even though between SU weekends away, camps, holidays, and visits to other churches I would not be able to attend every week.

The minister and his wife immediately embraced me and were anxious to ensure that I felt settled and cared for. Their two teenage sons also made me feel right at home; the boys made me laugh and immediately treated me almost like an older sister. One Sunday, I was invited to lunch at their house after church. No sooner had his mother served our main meal than the older boy (who was about eighteen) picked up the Brussels sprouts from his plate (with his fingers) and put them on mine, saying he didn't like them, so I could have them! His poor parents looked mortified that he should do such a thing to the 'new SU worker' despite my assurances that I now felt really at home and part of the family.

During the year, I became involved with several aspects of my minister's work – Religious Education classes in local schools; an end of year primary assembly; children's talks at church; a primary SU group and an after school SU group with my minster's wife; and an Easter holiday club. Although my limited health precluded me from involvement in other aspects of church life and I wasn't able to get to know a lot of people very well, a warm welcome and faithful prayer surrounded me. Here was the answer to my prayers for a temporary church family.

God delights in answering our prayers for the smallest of details that may seem totally insignificant in the grand scheme of things, but which are nevertheless important to us. Soon after I began work in the SU Glasgow office, the then-Director of Regional Staff asked if I could make use of a bike. Having recently purchased a new one, she thought her old one might be helpful to me. What had I prayed for in Australia as a possible mode of transport but a bike?

Because the congested city traffic combined with Scotland's inclement weather meant that a bike would not be a terribly practical mode of transport for me, I actually didn't use it. The incident nevertheless demonstrated that God had heard every little detail I had prayed about and was able to move people's hearts towards providing my needs even before I asked. The bike was a constant reminder of that as it lodged behind my desk in the office...it made a great hanger for my wet swimsuit and towel after periodic morning swim sessions with Fiona before work.

Many other gifts of various kinds further proved God's care. I hadn't personally asked for financial contributions towards the cost of my year and yet people gave at unexpected times and in wonderful ways from both Australia and Scotland.

My new church in Glasgow organised a couple of 'retiring offerings' for me where people were free to contribute as they were leaving the service. I was touched that I could be given so much by people who barely knew me but who were keen to support the work of SU Scotland that I had come to do. A couple of the other churches that I visited also gave gifts to help, and some anonymous donations were sent to the SU office. Before I had even arrived, Fiona had prepared an information brochure inviting people to pray and support my work. I was very humbled.

When Libby discovered my November birthday a celebration dinner party was organised and invitations issued to a few other girls from the SU office. Each one bought me a gift, and I was treated a fantastic three-course dinner to help me feel at home and not so lonely on my birthday.

Kathryn Kerridge

Although the concept of feeling freezing cold in the middle of summer amused many of the locals, sympathy abounded. Soon after my arrival, I arranged to meet up with a former camper from Lendrick Muir in 1999. We had kept in touch since then by letter; she and her family lived in Glasgow. Noticing how chilled I was, even inside the house, her mum immediately lit the fire in their living room so I could sit in front of it – although deliciously warm to me, sweat poured from everyone else in the room, but no one complained.

Buying more jumpers, trousers and cardigans was a good excuse for some shopping, and I wore thermal layers underneath these – yes, even in summer. Among my birthday and Christmas presents I received three scarves, two warm hats, and a pair of gloves. A couple of staff in the Glasgow office offered me warm clothes that they didn't need, and my friend Sandy from Montana sent me a package of thermals. On another occasion, a lovely goose-down lined outdoor jacket arrived from her in the post. She didn't want me to be cold while telling the Scottish kids about Jesus, her accompanying card said.

God provided so much love, support and friendship for me – those intangible things so vital to my soul in times of loneliness and homesickness. There were difficult times of intensely missing my family, friends and home country, especially in the dark winter months and at times when my health declined. It was sometimes a challenge to remember why I was here in the first place. For strength and comfort I was driven to press more closely into God's Word and into His presence as I cried many tears to Him in prayer.

Those first few months encompassed many tests of faith. The most obvious one was in terms of my health. I had arrived in Scotland one week prior to the fortnight of Year Team training to recover from jet lag, meet with some SU staff, and generally settle in.

The two-day, predominantly sleepless journey from Australia had been arduous and I spent the next week trying to adjust my body to the nine-hour time difference and the jet-lag that flattened me. By the time I arrived at Year Team training, I was already flagging energy-wise, and there were two intense weeks ahead of me – full days and evenings of Bible teaching sessions and seminars to prepare us for our year.

As well as absorbing a mountain of information, the other nine members of the team and I were building relationships with each other, after being quickly thrust into close living quarters and shared responsibilities. The other members of the group ranged in age from seventeen to twenty-four (and yes, I felt like a bit of a 'grandma' at almost thirty-two!). In addition to six Scottish young people, there was a girl from Latvia, a girl from Austria, and myself.

Two days into training I had already worked more hours than what I would normally work in a week in the library and I was physically shattered. Added to fatigue was the process of fully coming to terms with the fact that I was here for a whole year, had no family and friends around me, and was feeling so darn freezing cold *all* the time, indoors and out. I was already craving the glaringly bright Aussie sunshine, and if this was a Scottish summer, I wondered if I would ever feel warm again before the year was out.

I found myself wondering, 'What have I done, and what on earth am I doing in Scotland?' As I was reading my Bible during a morning quiet time, it was as if God was plainly answering from the words of a passage in Isaiah:-

> *'I took you from the ends of the earth,*
> *from its farthest corners I called you.*
> *I said, 'You are my servant';*
> *I have chosen you and have not rejected you.*
> *So do not fear, for I am with you;*
> *do not be dismayed, for I am your God.*
> *I will strengthen you and help you;*
> *I will uphold you with my righteous right hand.'*
> *(Isaiah 41:9-10 NIV)*

I was stunned at how accurately God had addressed my situation with those ancient words. Thinking of a globe of the world and the locations of Brisbane, Australia and Glasgow, Scotland, He really had taken me 'from the ends of the earth'. The confirmation of His call was plain, as was the reassurance of His strength, help and presence. My instructions were plain, too – I was not to fear and not to be dismayed. In the year that followed, I would turn to these words again and again in times of pressure, to feel my spirit receive renewed courage and the strength to go on in His calling, even though I had no idea where it was leading.

God had yet to sort out a few things with me in this training period so that I would be able to last the distance. He well knew my driven and stubborn tendencies that, unchecked, would lead to my downfall before I even began.

Despite the obvious weakness of my health, I felt I could ask for no special favours. I was part of this team on an equal basis with the other young people who were not all finding it easy either, so I had to grit my teeth, push my body and get on with it. I was so blessed by the love and support shown by the other members of my team; although I was the oldest by far, I often felt that they were the ones looking out for me, asking if I was okay and if they could do anything for me, my roommates tiptoeing around my bed when I used my spare time to nap for a precious hour or so.

Despite my best efforts, I was desperately tired, and began to panic about my body collapsing before I had even finished training. Perhaps I had made the biggest mistake of my life by committing to this seemingly impossible task. It was not fair that I had promised SU Scotland a year that I would not be able to deliver on. The heaviness of my heart was compounded by the fact that I loved the Bible teaching and worship times, and was so excited about what we were learning. I *hated* being too exhausted to fully focus and to give myself as completely as I desired to building relationships with the other members of my team, who had such wonderful gifts and hearts to serve God.

One afternoon, we piled into the minibus for a surprise excursion to Aviemore, the little Highland resort town near Alltnacriche, the SU outdoor centre at which we were based for training. The surprise was a couple of hours at the go-kart track. We donned helmets to spend some time roaring round the track to let off some steam and give our brains a break from all the seminars.

As I got the hang of driving my little kart, my speed increased and I started racing with two of the boys. Soon after, I took a bend way too sharply and crashed into the barrier at full speed. The impact winded me and I was unable to move my legs to reverse and drive my kart off the track. My knees hurt so much that I was sure I had smashed them, and all I could think was that I was living in a third floor flat, and how was I going to manage all the stairs with a broken leg (or two)?

From the Ends of the Earth

The track attendant came to my rescue, and rightly berated me for driving too fast. Breathing a heartfelt prayer of thanks, I was relieved to find that I was able to climb out of the go-kart with my legs both in one piece, and sit on the bleachers. The object lesson couldn't have been clearer. God may have called me here and promised to provide me with all the strength I needed to get through, but I would have to pay very close attention to my body, use wisdom with my energy, and be prepared to ask for help or extra rest when I needed it; otherwise I would be heading for a severe crash.

I wasn't the only one who spotted the lesson in this. Later, back at Alltnacriche, one of the Year Team programme leaders cornered me in the kitchen for a chat about how I was planning to deal with the year and my health. His purpose was clearly not to disparage me for my physical limitations but to truly voice his concern that I stay healthy to do what God had called me to do, and to assure me of the support of all involved in the programme.

Another member of the leadership group, a former SU staff worker, approached me one day during a coffee break. Sitting beside me, her first question was, 'Will you let us help you?' Touched, I realised that my perfectionist tendencies were really a matter of pride. I had come to another country to work and live among people that I didn't know and who didn't know me and my first response was to try to be superhuman and do everything brilliantly so they wouldn't regret accepting my application. I had to be humble enough to accept my limitations and ask for help from these loving and godly people who were just waiting to assist in any way they could.

I did not have to try to make up for what I truly was not able to physically do, but I did have to take responsibility for being wise with my health. God had clearly placed me under the authority of astute and thoughtful Christians who cared deeply about the welfare of their volunteers – physically, mentally and spiritually. I was going to be fine this year, whatever lay ahead.

In the Bible teaching during this first week of training, we studied the lives and ministries of Moses, Elijah, Gideon, David and Paul. The recurring theme was clearly that God often chooses not the strongest, healthiest, most talented people to accomplish His purposes. He chooses to use us with all our weaknesses, insecurities and past failures because in our inabilities, His strength is most clearly demonstrated. He searches primarily not for talent but for hearts that desire to follow Him and be used by Him.

Midway through training, we were introduced to the wider work of SU and a huge number of other staff and faithful supporters at the 'Big Celebration'. This annual event was held at the end of each summer, primarily to give thanks for the summer camp season, and to unite SU supporters, volunteers, and staff from all over Scotland for fun, food, prayer and a worship service. A number of seminar sessions were also available, one of which was entitled 'So You Want To Work For SU?'

Well, I had come to Scotland on a one-way plane ticket on God's leading and had wondered before I even arrived whether the purpose of my doing the Year Team programme might be subsequent schools' work, so I considered attending. Would it look too presumptuous when I had only been 'with SU' on the gap year programme for one week? As I mentally pondered this, another of the Year Team girls, Michelle, said that she was thinking about going along so we went together, feeling a little self-conscious and grateful for each other's company. I learnt more about SU Scotland, but wasn't struck with a strong sense one way or another as to whether God would take me in that direction after this year.

As the months passed, I settled into my role with SU in a wonderful variety of ministry opportunities with children and young people - school assemblies, SU groups, conferences for senior high pupils, training events for volunteers, holiday camps, and events at churches – occasions that had me travelling to many different parts of Scotland.

God was certainly knitting together all my years of experience. I was working with children and adults of all ages in such a variety of contexts that I could clearly see how and why God had prepared me and called me to serve this year with SU Scotland.

Longer term I still had no idea what all this was leading to or what the one-way plane ticket was all about. Once I had become sure of God's leading in this strange little adventure, I had been quite willing to leave my Australian life behind for a year and leave the next steps to Him, but by now I had been expecting some sort of guidance as to what that might be.

Most of those whom I met knew that my time in Scotland was open-ended as I gave the honest answer of 'I don't know' whenever I was asked how long I was going to be in Scotland and what I was going to do after Year Team. That was fine, even quite exciting for the first half of the year – in fact, God often used the situation as an opportunity to share my faith. Many young people asked questions about why I came from Australia to Scotland and how I was able to trust God to lead me into what was next. I was glad to be demonstrating an example of the kind of faith and trust that a Christian is called to have, and is able to have in a faithful and loving God who has a plan for our lives and guides us into that plan in His perfect timing. It was also an example to the other young people on my Year Team, as many were similarly 'in the dark' about what to do after the year was over.

From the Ends of the Earth

At our mid-year training in early January, the issue of 'life after Year Team' arose in our individual interviews. In one sense, it wasn't a great concern as I had a job and a life to resume back home, but the one-way plane ticket meant being open to the possibility that God might want me to stay on. The expected clear conviction one way or the other didn't come. Some days I would be quite happy to stay in Scotland; other days I would desperately want the year to fly by as quickly as possible so I could go home to my life and friends. The picture in my mind was of a set of old-fashioned scales…sometimes they tipped one way, sometimes the other – but the end result was always an even balance.

God continued to look after me, though, proving that what was unknown to me was fully known to Him. My accommodation at Libby's was only available for four months; after that I would need accommodation elsewhere. I wasn't too worried about this, as although I was praying about it, it was SU's responsibility to find me somewhere else to live. As the months went by and December loomed, nothing had eventuated, and I became concerned that my next 'home' had still not been found.

Just in time, accommodation was found with a single lady who was an SU volunteer. Once again, God had provided all my needs. I had a cosy room of my own in a comfortable little house, the independence of doing my own shopping and cooking and coming and going as I liked, and proximity to shops and public transport. Best of all, I had the company of a generous and caring Christian woman, Pam, who would bless me with her faith, advice, encouragement and service to God. She, too, had done overseas mission work, so could identify with some of my struggles, and she too was going through a period of transition job-wise, awaiting God's direction and provision in some similar ways to myself. Many uplifting heart-to-heart conversations were had over cups of tea as we curled up in her comfortable lounge chairs.

For the first Christmas I had ever spent away from my family, I was adopted into Fiona's at their home in Edinburgh. I was so warmly welcomed and included that there was no chance to feel homesick. There were presents for me under the tree, and I enjoyed my first-ever hot turkey Christmas dinner. Quite a contrast to a Queensland Christmas lunch which was usually celebrated in thirty-plus degree heat with lots of ice-cold drinks, salads, cold meats or seafood, ice cream and watermelon, sometimes after a swim at the beach to cool off after church. A Boxing Day stroll along the beach at St Andrews with Fiona's family had me warmly cocooned in a sheepskin-lined jacket, scarf, gloves, wool socks and boots. No bare feet in the sand this time.

Just in case God did call me to stay in Scotland, I researched what I might possibly do and how much I needed to earn to afford to live there. Although I had originally wondered if God might be leading me towards regional staff work for SU, within a couple of months of experiencing the demands of the job, I knew that it required a level of good health and stamina that I clearly did not have. Even sticking to part-time hours sometimes proved difficult and there was a lack of the kind of routine that my body needed in the longer term. So much for that idea – it seemed that one wasn't from God after all.

As I occasionally flicked through the newspaper to look at jobs and accommodation, it took very little time to realise that I could not earn enough working only part-time to afford rent and food, let alone anything else. If God did want me to stay He would have to He would have to arrange something extraordinary because it certainly looked to be impossible.

Despite my best efforts to limit myself to working part-time (and with huge amounts of help and understanding from SU staff), the often irregular hours of work combined with the stress of the cold and dreary climate, homesickness and loneliness for my family and closest friends were gradually eroding the health that had taken the past decade to stabilise. It was sometimes difficult not to succumb to fear of an ME relapse, and yet I just couldn't believe that God would so clearly bring me into a situation which would lead to such a devastating end.

I had no choice but to keep going one day at a time, focusing on the verses from Isaiah 41 that had so encouraged me at Year Team training, and trusting Him for my future even though I couldn't understand His process.

Dad suffered a serious fall in February 2003, the news of which added to the stress of being so far from home. While fixing something on the church roof, he fell from a ladder onto a tiled area, the impact of which could easily have proved fatal. He narrowly missed hitting his head and badly broke his right arm and shoulder. Unable to move at all and lying in the rain, he was miraculously noticed by a woman passing by who called the ambulance.

For ten weeks, Dad was not allowed to lie down at all, even to sleep, because his arm had to be maintained in a certain position as the bones healed. He underwent surgery to insert a metal pin and it was uncertain whether he would regain full use of his arm and hand or suffer permanent nerve damage. For my robust and healthy farmer father, the pain, fatigue and helplessness he was suffering was horrendous for me to imagine.

Obviously, this was a very difficult time for my Mum too, as she had to do everything for Dad – bathing, dressing, feeding, and driving him – and helplessly watch him suffering in pain. All I wanted to do was jump on a plane and go home, not hear weekly reports over the phone from thousands of miles away, but I could not. One of the costs of following the will of God for my life was not being nearby in times of crisis (although of course I would have flown home if Dad's condition was life-threatening).

Thankfully Dad's arm and shoulder had healed almost perfectly four months later. He regained the strength in his muscles and full use of his arm and fingers, and now has only a long scar and a slightly bent elbow as a reminder to always have someone at the bottom of the ladder holding it steady.

More months passed and still I waited for some indication from God as to what I should do next. Sometimes I fought impatience at the 'lack of information' that I felt God was providing – I had grown used to following His lead on short notice over the past few years, but my natural inclination was still towards forward planning far in advance. I had learned that God will not be rushed; in the waiting time I had to keep my focus on what lay before me just then and be open to either going or staying afterwards.

A Christian bookstore in Glasgow was a favourite lunch break destination where I could listen to the latest CDs and browse the books. One day, a Celtic-style CD caught my eye.

Listening to the songs on the store's CD player, I followed along the lyric sheet until I came to one song in particular. It spoke of the challenge of trusting God when the future is unknown and when following Him involves leaving behind a homeland, family, security and all that one knows and loves. Acknowledging the tears, fears and questions that are part of the natural human response, the words could not possibly have been more appropriate to my situation, and it felt as if the song was written just for me.

I had to switch off the CD then and there lest I become a blubbering mess in the middle of the bookstore! Without hesitation I bought the CD and in song after song, God spoke words of comfort, encouragement and love to my questioning soul.

Throughout all of my years of 'missionary journeys' I was well aware that God might call me to leave my homeland for good one day, but never had the implications of that prospect impacted more deeply than now.

In the eyes of some, I lived an enviable life flitting all over the world at a moment's notice, and in many respects it was exhilarating, exciting and rewarding. Naturally I was thrilled that I was finally able to 'spread my wings and fly' after years of life-limiting illness. However, the cold reality of living half a world away from family and friends, not to mention the sun, white sandy beaches and long hot summers of Queensland, was sobering and daunting. It was certainly possible that God might be asking this of me once my Year Team time was over. This was indeed the question I faced, but one to which I had no definite answer…yet.

From the Ends of the Earth

At the beginning of May 2003, I joined my SU colleagues at Lendrick Muir for two days of staff training. This occurred three times each year and I always looked forward to the event – the schools' workers were mostly around my age and were a vital social link for me apart from anything else.

On the morning of the second day, I arose early as usual to have my quiet time with God and an early morning walk. The signs of spring and the increasing hours of daylight breathed new life to my soul after the darkness and barrenness of winter. Walking beside Rumbling Bridge Gorge, I pondered and prayed about what to do after Year Team.

My official time with the schools' work option would end on June 30 at the conclusion of the school year, although I was planning to stay into the summer to assist Fiona in leading SU's Creative Arts Camp. However, a decision needed to be made now about whether to return to Australia afterwards. If I was going home, the leave from my job expired at the beginning of August so I would need to buy a plane ticket as soon as possible. If I was going to stay in Scotland, I needed to resign properly so that a replacement could be found with minimal disruption to the YPLS programme.

My conclusion was that although I had been prepared to stay in Scotland if God asked me to, I hadn't seen any specific opportunity that I was supposed to take up, and therefore I would be going home after the summer.

Completely at peace with that decision, excitement rose at the thought of seeing my family and friends again in just a few months time. All sorted – or so I thought.

After my walk, I went to the kitchen to make a cup of coffee to drink during my quiet time. As I was standing at the urn, pouring hot water, who should walk into the room but one of the Year Team supervisors. This was the same man who had cornered me at training for a chat following my little go-kart accident, and who had given me wise advice at other times during the year.

His question was whether I had decided what to do after Year Team. I explained I had just then concluded that I would return to Australia as I didn't see another clear path that I felt God wanted me to take in Scotland. Mysteriously, I was told that the Lendrick Muir Centre Director wished to speak to me later that day.

A couple of hours afterwards, I was approached with a proposal that blew my mind. Due to some restructuring, SU was looking for a new gap year programme co-ordinator to be based at Lendrick Muir. The role would encompass pastoral care of the team on a day-to-day basis, as well as administrative and recruitment duties.

From the Ends of the Earth

As the job was being described, I had an incredibly strong impression that this was the reason God had brought me to Scotland. I was stunned at the timing – only a couple of hours previously I had decided that it was right to return home, and now this! What was going on?

Although almost positive that my answer to this job offer would be 'yes', I asked for time to think and pray it through. Mum and Dad were phoned that night and joined me in prayer.

Later that evening I sat down with pen and paper. The job certainly sounded right but there were some practical considerations. I listed my questions and the requirements that I felt were reasonable – manageable working hours, income, transport off-site, and freedom to continue with SU's children's work and training opportunities as I still felt that my gifts lay primarily in those areas.

Questions aside, so many previously puzzling aspects of my year were falling into place – the reason I had come on a one-way ticket was because I was meant to stay; the reason I had been called to the Year Team programme was so that I could co-ordinate it and help future participants through it; the reason I was doing a gap-year at thirty-two years of age was so that I had the work experience and spiritual maturity to take on the role of discipling and caring for a team of teenagers and young adults; the reason God had brought me from Australia with all my travel experience was so that I could easily help care for international year team members who might struggle with the cultural and climate change, homesickness etc.

What I had originally thought was an illogical path turned out to be far from random; although it did seem as though God had left it to the last minute to reveal it to me. However, I had to smile – even as I had begged Him to tell me further in advance what I was to do, it would have made no sense for Him to do so. Because the revamp of the job description and hours was so recent, the opportunity God had been preparing me for didn't even exist when I arrived in Scotland. In fact, it didn't exist until just before I was told about it. He wasn't giving me information too late, but right on time.

As these revelations swirled through my head, I felt speechless to ponder the amazing detail and perfection of God's plan. How He must have chuckled at my amazement when I finally understood what He had been planning all along.

The sense that this was 'my job' was further confirmed when I met with the Lendrick Muir Centre Director the following day. By the time she had explained the job and its terms and conditions more fully, I had crossed off every single question I had jotted down. As she spoke, I had been ticking them off one by one until there were no issues left to raise.

From the Ends of the Earth

God had taken care of every practical detail, and I knew the job was mine.

With that, I went to compose an email to Jen to resign from my library post. With mixed feelings I typed – I was sad to leave a job I loved so much, especially since I really didn't know quite what I was in for with this new one, but I felt a deep assurance that I was doing the right thing.

A new era of my life was about to begin, although at the time I told SU that I would try the job for a year and see what happened. Little did I know that after that year I would stay for another....and another....and another...and more! A huge, and by no means easy, learning curve lay ahead so maybe it was just as well God didn't reveal at that point how long I would remain in Scotland.

I finished off my own Year Team year in Glasgow concurrently with starting my new job; my unexpected career change had begun.

Kathryn Kerridge

Chapter 18

As I badly needed a break between the end of my own gap year and training the new team, I took a week off to fly south and visit Burgess Hill, the birthplace of my grandmother and mother.

Mum had continued writing to an old school friend for the previous fifty years, and I was able to stay with her. In Burgess Hill also lived one of Mum's cousins and his wife.

I hadn't much considered my English heritage before, except for the fact that I was able to now live in the UK because Mum was born there. However, as she had been in Australia since the age of fifteen, she had no English accent left and her once-fair English skin had long been tanned by the harsh Australian sun. To me she had always been just a normal Aussie mum. Apart from a couple of Mum's cousins, there had long since ceased to be relatives living in England.

However, as I wandered around Burgess Hill and contemplated my new job and home in Scotland, I was heavily struck by the detailed design of God in placing me into my family, and how He was using aspects of my heritage in my life right now.

From the Ends of the Earth

It was here in Burgess Hill that my grandmother was born in 1905. It was here that she grew up with her mother, father, brothers and sisters and attended school, Sunday School and church. It was here that she became a Christian and as a young teenager sensed God calling her to the mission field. It was here that she went 'into service' after leaving school at thirteen to help earn money for the family. It was here in Burgess Hill that God continued to train, teach and prepare my grandmother for missionary service in China. Standing in front of the house in which she had lived, I thought how amazed she would be, had she been alive, to see that one of her granddaughters had been called to be a missionary in Britain (not that I'm saying that England and Scotland are the same, of course!)

In this same house Mum was born during her parents' furlough from China, hence my entitlement to a 'Right of Abode to the UK'. This was how I could travel to Scotland on a one-way ticket and decide to accept a further job with no need for any immigration procedures. In fact, I could come and go between Australia and the UK as I pleased – or rather, as God led me – and here I was almost a hundred years after the birth of my grandmother knowing that He had not only ordained and planned her birth, but that of my mother, and also that of me.

I was catching a glimpse of how difficult it must have been for Mum to leave England at the age of fifteen, not knowing when or if she would ever return. As I contemplated not returning home in the near future, I empathised with young Margaret having to leave family, friends, familiar landscape and her culture to make a new life in a country on the other side of the world as my grandmother had done when she sailed to China in 1930 at the age of twenty-five. God had given me the examples of two wonderful godly women who had preceded me. He had looked after, provided for and blessed them, and would do the same for me. What an incredible family history I was privileged to be part of and although I couldn't see how my life fit together at times, how could I doubt that no detail had been forgotten?

Reflecting on my life, I can see many themes consistently flowing through it that illustrate God's methods in our lives. As I have come to understand the character and the processes of God more deeply through my personal experiences of Him, my faith is strengthened and the path of faith becomes easier to tread, even when all is not going well.

God will allow us to go through whatever it takes, however difficult the circumstances, to make us into the people He wants us to be. He is far less concerned with our achievements than our character, and the truth is that character, endurance and strength are best forged in the furnace of suffering. He is always present and walking with us in our trials and will use them for His glory and our benefit if we submit to the work He wants to do in us. The 'bad news' is that these times are usually painful, but the great news is that nothing we go through in life is wasted when we look at life from God's perspective. We can feel ourselves getting stronger with each test we pass; more Christ-like as God refines our character; and more able to relate to, and empathise with, the people around us, whether or not they know God themselves. I cannot count the number of times that the topic of my illness has opened up opportunities to share with people all over the world my faith and my testimony of God's faithfulness in life's darkest times as well as in life's joys.

Furthermore no circumstance, disaster or disability can prevent God from using us or positioning us where He wants us to be. I find this one of the wonderfully comforting facts about being a Christian. The world usually rewards the talented, the wealthy, the smart, the healthy, the beautiful; in short, the outward appearances. God looks only for a heart that is willing to serve Him, love Him and trust Him, and with that, He can do anything. I am surely the least likely choice of person to do what God has called me to do. It boggles my mind to think why God would choose a simple Australian girl from Brisbane with a chronic health condition to travel the world for Him, but He has. One thing is for certain…it's not about me; it's all about Him - *His* power, *His* strength, *His* calling, *His* grace, *His* gifts, and His love and concern for my life. Nothing in the external circumstances of our lives discounts us from being used by God; in fact, time and time again the Scriptures reveal that He deliberately chooses the least likely candidates to do His work – that way, more glory goes to Him.

Daily I am reminded through the blessings of God that if we seek first His kingdom and make that our primary concern, He is faithful to provide our needs and many other blessings besides. I would be lying if I said that I never had moments of fear about my future as I live this rather 'unconventional' life. However, I have consistently known God's supply of my needs, be they material or social or emotional or spiritual. My responsibility is to follow wholeheartedly the path that God sets before me, and to use wisely the gifts and possessions He enables me to have. The rest I leave to Him as His responsibility, to fulfil His promises of care and provision for me.

Life is rarely a smooth ride for anyone. Along with joys, achievements and successes, there are deep valleys of disappointment, disaster and despair. Not one of us can possibly have total control over our lives, no matter how much we might like to think we do. We never know what is coming around the corner for good or for evil, but I can think of no way I'd rather live my life than to leave it in the hands of the God who made me, created the universe, and has more power and more knowledge than I can ever imagine. God knows exactly where I am at any moment and what I am going through; He knows exactly what the future holds for me and He loves me more than I can comprehend. And when this topsy-turvy passage of life is over, I have the security of an eternity in heaven with Him – free of pain, tears, disappointment, sorrow, fear, sickness or death. That's a hope I'd stake my life on.

"Now to Him who is able to do immeasurably more than all we ask or imagine, according to His power that is at work within us, to Him be the glory in the church and in Christ Jesus throughout all generations, forever and ever! Amen" (Ephesians 3:20-21; NIV)

Kathryn Kerridge

Epilogue

January 2010 – Seven and a half years after flying to Scotland on that one-way ticket in August 2002, I am back in Brisbane at my parents' home for a long summer break.

I had accepted the Gap Year Co-ordinator job on a 'give it a go for a year' basis, not knowing whether I would like it or be any good at it, without any idea that one year would turn into many more. Particularly in the first couple of years, I often wondered whether God wasn't mistaken in putting me, rather than a qualified and experienced youth worker, in the position. However, His call to me remained clear and constant throughout all that time and He doesn't make mistakes - each year I sensed Him clearly say, 'Stay another year', so I did.

As my years in the job continued, I began to see how He had been equipping me all my life to fulfil that calling, especially, it seemed, through my law studies at University. Problem-solving, mediation, imparting wise counsel, listening, evaluating situations, conflict resolution, impartiality – the skills I had learned then were being put to good use. I even played the role of a 'judge' of sorts on many occasions. My law degree had not been a mistake or a waste – God makes use of everything, just not always in the way we envision.

From the Ends of the Earth

After working with gap year participants for five and a half years, God led me to once again minister predominantly to children. I moved north to Alltnacriche, SU's residential outdoor centre in the Scottish Highlands, to work with primary school groups.

As I sift through letters, photo albums, gifts and travel mementoes shipped from Scotland, my mind is transported back over an incredible seven and a half years. God's blessings to me have extended far beyond Britain's borders.

In addition to holidays in Australia during that time, I have travelled to more countries than I ever dreamed I would. There have been ministry opportunities in Lithuania and Hungary, reunions with American friends in Ireland and Denmark, holidays with Australian friends in Italy and Holland, the wedding of friends in Latvia, travels with Scottish friends to Mallorca, Cyprus, Italy, Spain, Poland, Austria, France and Switzerland, visits to the home of a friend in Northern Ireland and a pen pal in Germany. My parents were able to come to Scotland one summer, and together we travelled to the Czech Republic.

Christmas 2006 was spent in India at the home of my friend Sylvia, a colleague from Lendrick Muir. As I sat in church with her family on Christmas Eve, dressed in a beautiful silk sari, I was overwhelmed to realise that in the previous twelve months alone, I had worshipped with other Christians in churches in Australia, Northern Ireland, Germany, Hungary, many different parts of Scotland and now India.

Just as with my trips to the USA, many of these travel opportunities arose quite unexpectedly and without striving on my part. They were like gifts from God at just the right times, with the right people, in a way which I could afford. Page after page of my passport filled with stamps, each one representing a separate story of God's love and provision and attention to detail.

I won't be in Australia for long. My new passport is full of blank pages, and I will soon return to Scotland to continue working with SU until the end of October 2010. After that, who knows? I don't, but God does, and that's exciting. Watch this space…